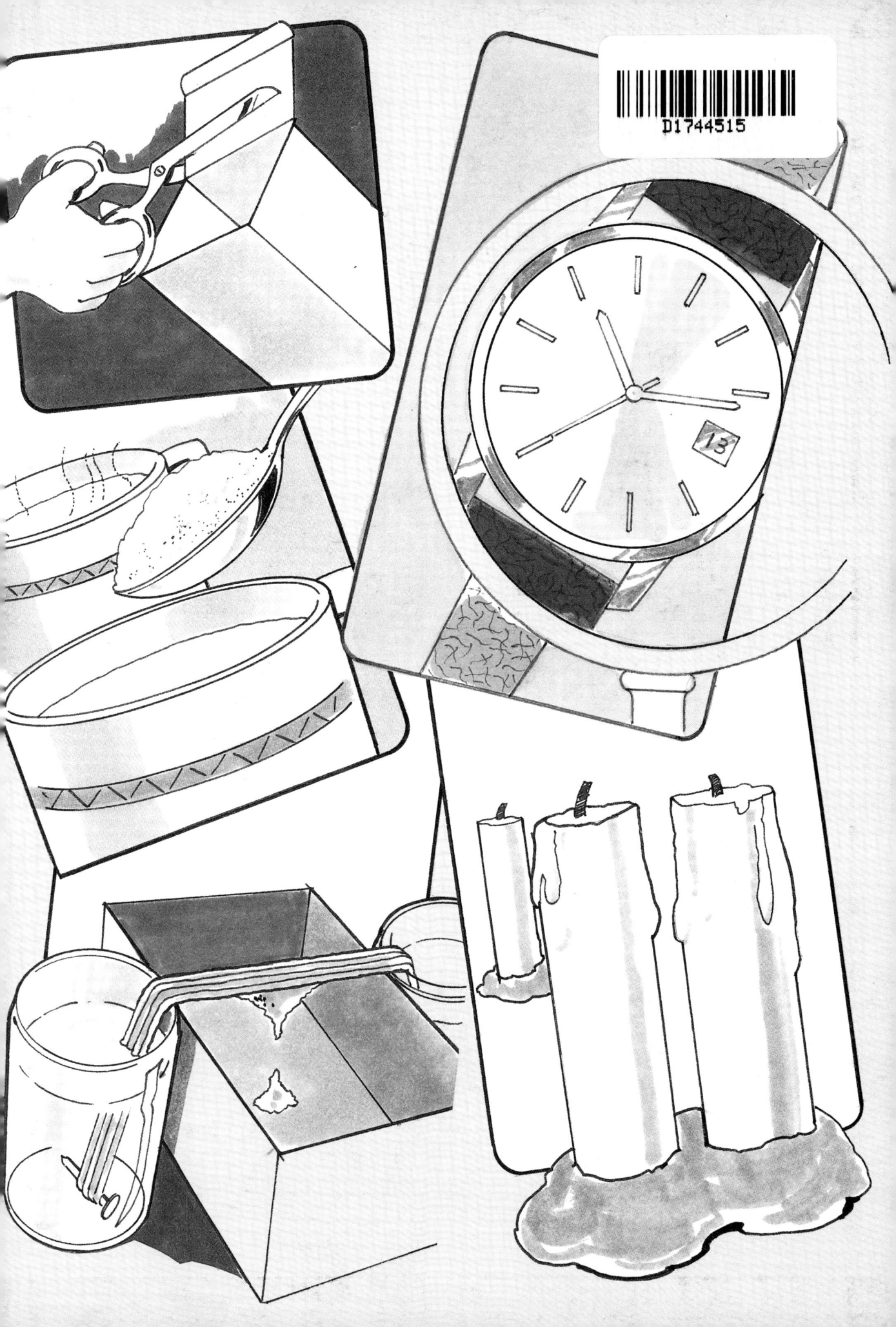

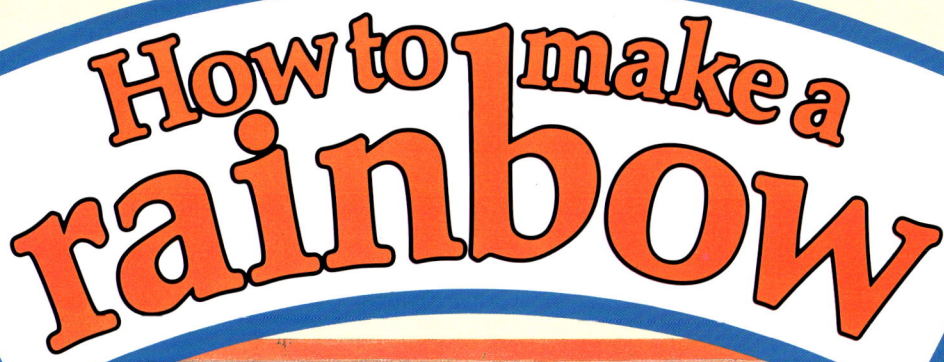

How to make a rainbow

Illustrated by
Terry Riley

Compiled by
Derek Hall

Hamlyn
London · New York
Sydney · Toronto

Published 1984 by
The Hamlyn Publishing Group Limited
London . New York . Sydney . Toronto
Astronaut House, Feltham, Middlesex, England
© Copyright 1984 The Hamlyn Publishing Group
Limited

ISBN 0 600 38922 7

Printed in Italy

Contents

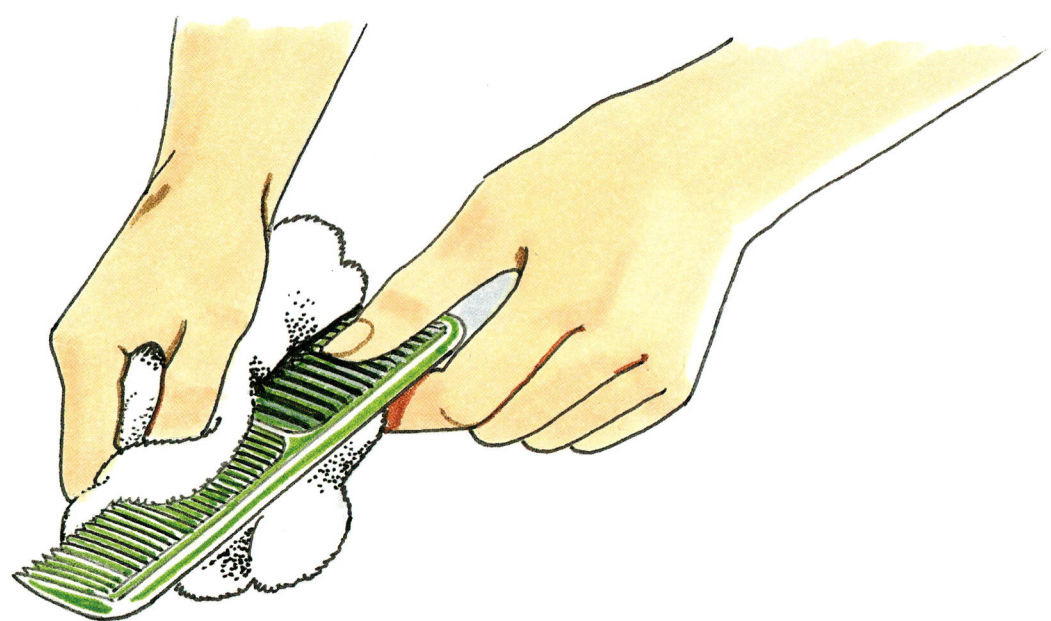

Introduction

This book will show you that science is not only a fascinating subject, but that it can be great fun, too. Most of the experiments can be performed inside the home but sometimes we suggest doing certain ones outside, and you will see why! There are also lots of models to make and even some tricks you can do to amaze your friends.

The principles behind most of the experiments are explained briefly so that once you have done the experiment you can often make up more experiments of your own.

Almost all of the experiments can be carried out using simple household items such as paper, thread, pieces of wood and wire. Other items which are sometimes necessary, such as magnets, you may have to buy if you have not already got them but they are all cheap and easy to find. It is a good idea to keep all the items in a large cardboard or wooden box, for many things can be used for several of the experiments. If you keep them together you will not have to go on a search before you begin each experiment.

To help you identify the plants and animals discussed in some of the experiments, go to your local library or bookseller for a selection of suitable books.

Do not be discouraged if, occasionally, an experiment does not seem to work. Try again. It is sometimes necessary to adjust the set up or even to start again from the beginning in order to get the conditions just right.

Safety

Watch out for this sign ☆. You will need to ask an adult to help you with any experiment that has this sign, and they must be present throughout the experiment. Make sure you have permission from an adult before doing *any* experiment, and be sure that there is always an adult nearby to help if needed.

Be extremely careful with lighted candles. You must always get an adult to light candles for you, and be sure to do any experiments using candles on a fireproof surface. Take special care when handling glass objects. If you need a tin can, use one that has a lid because one that has been opened with a tin opener will have dangerous sharp edges. Don't touch anything that is hot, and always wash your hands after handling things like moth balls, any chemicals, and toadstools.

It is a good idea to wear an apron when doing experiments, to protect your clothes. Any experiment using water should be done over a sink or outside the house. It is very dangerous to leave things lying about, so make certain that you always clear up after doing any experiments. Everything should be put away safely where it won't be stood on or tripped over. Be especially careful to pick up all knives, pins, nails, glass objects, and tin cans.

Good Experimenting!

Take fingerprints

The outer layer of the skin of the fingers forms a series of ridges. These enable us to hold objects without them slipping from our grasp. They are also a very useful feature for identifying people, for everyone's fingerprint is slightly different. Here is an easy way to record your fingerprint.

You Will Need
A soft lead pencil (marked B or 2B)
White paper
Transparent sticky tape

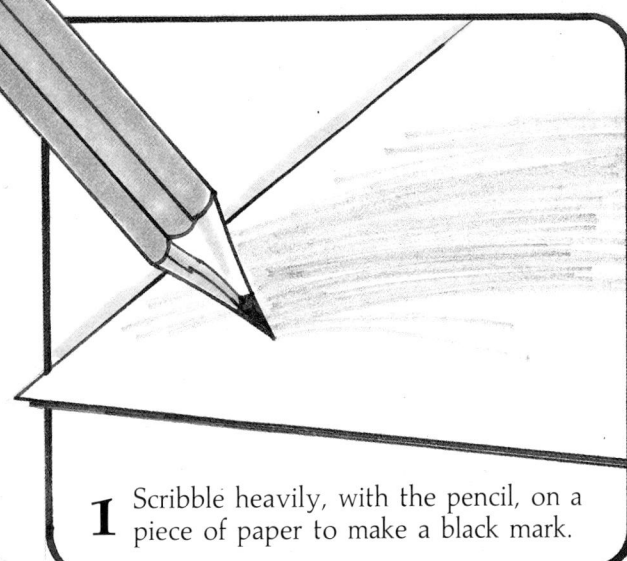

1 Scribble heavily, with the pencil, on a piece of paper to make a black mark.

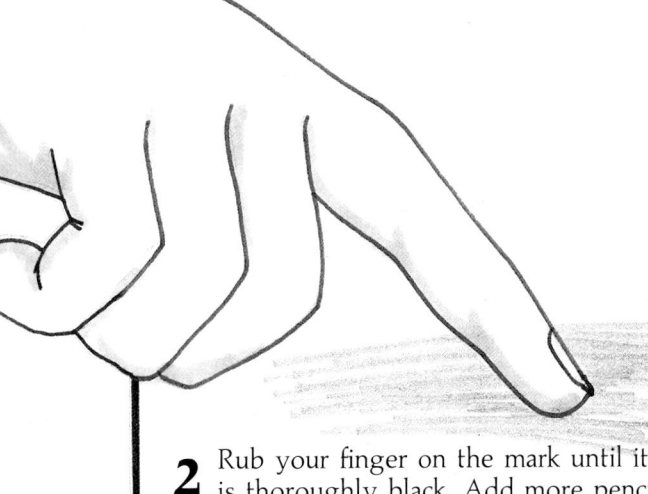

2 Rub your finger on the mark until it is thoroughly black. Add more pencil rubbing to the paper if necessary.

3 When your finger is black carefully press it on to the sticky side of a piece of the sticky tape, making sure that you do not touch the print afterwards. The ridges will show up as a finger print.

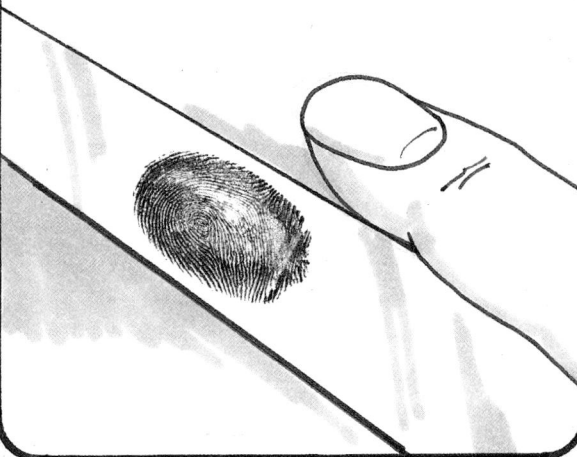

4 Turn the tape over and stick it to a piece of white paper to protect the print. Do all your fingers in turn.

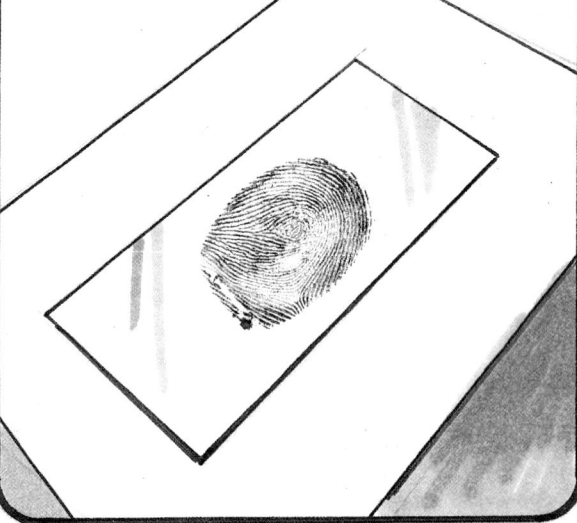

Make prints of your friends' and family's fingers and label them. Using a magnifying glass if necessary, see if you can spot differences between the various fingerprints.

Listen to your heartbeat

Would you like to hear your own heartbeat? You can make an instrument almost the same as the one which a doctor uses to listen to heartbeats. It is called a *stethoscope*.

You Will Need
3 small metal funnels
Y-piece (a common piece of plumbing equipment)
3 pieces of rubber or plastic tubing each about 60 cm long
Sticky tape
A friend

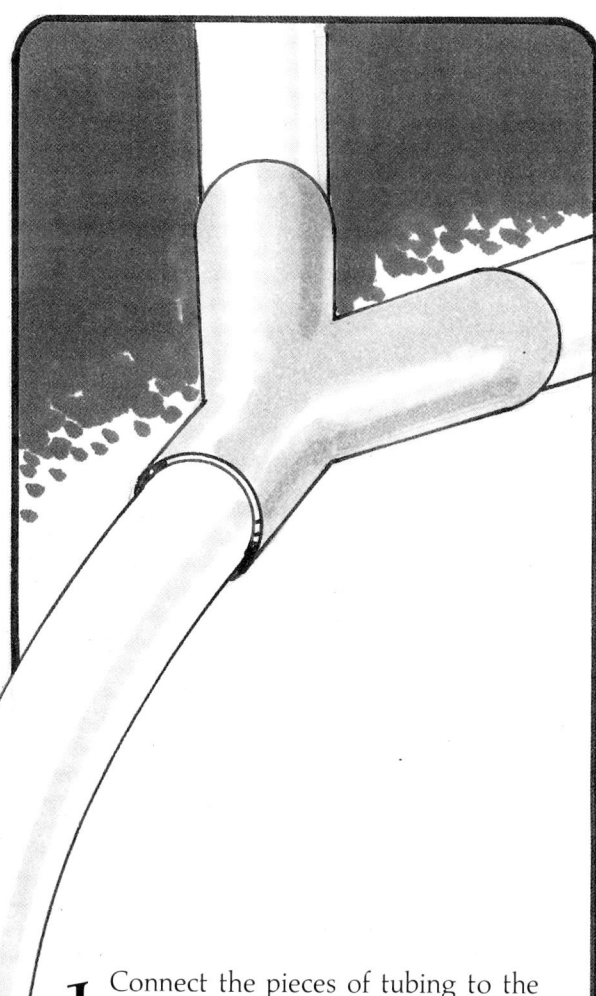

1 Connect the pieces of tubing to the Y-piece and the funnels, as shown, either by pushing them over the ends or by taping them if they do not fit snugly.

2 Get a friend to hold two of the funnels to your ears whilst you hold the other against your heart. Count the number of beats in a minute.

3 Run about for a few minutes, and count again. How long is it until your heart returns to its original number of beats? Listen to your friend's heart too and count the beats.

Your heart will beat faster when you run around because your body needs lots of oxygen to make energy. Oxygen is taken from your lungs and carried, in your blood, round your body. Your heart beats faster to pump the blood round your body more quickly.

Make a map of your tongue

Small organs, called taste buds, are located just below the surface of the tongue and at three places in the throat. Certain materials taken into the mouth cause the taste buds to produce the sensation of taste. Taste sensations may be divided into sweet, salty, sour and bitter.

The sense of taste is complicated by the fact that certain tastes are actually odours. This is true of the taste of an onion. If a bad cold causes you to lose your sense of smell, you will not be able to taste an onion.

The same buds do not detect all tastes.

Here is a way to make a map of your tongue to learn where the taste buds are.

You Will Need
4 Saucers
4 Spoons
A mirror
Paper
A pencil
Salt
Sugar
Coffee powder
Lemon juice
Water

**Sugar is sweet; salt is salty;
lemon juice is sour; and coffee is bitter.**

1 Put each of these taste materials into a separate saucer.

2 Dissolve the salt, sugar and coffee in a small amount of water, making strong solutions of each.

3 Dip the tip of a teaspoon into the sugar solution and place a very small amount on your tongue. Make sure you recognize a sweet taste, then rinse your mouth with water.

4 Using a separate teaspoon for each, put small amounts of the other taste materials on your tongue to make sure that you recognize each taste. Be sure to rinse your mouth between each tasting.

7 Look in the mirror, to see on which part of your tongue you put the sugar solution. If you recognize a sweet taste, mark on the drawing that represents your tongue the letters SW to show where you could taste sweet. Do this again on several different places on your tongue, marking on the drawing each time you note a sweet taste. When you have finished, you will have mapped where the tongue has taste buds that sense sweetness.

5 Draw an outline like the one in the illustration. This represents your tongue.

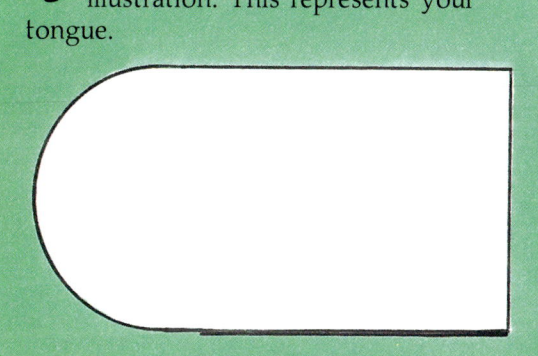

8 Using the solutions for salty, sour and bitter tastes, map the taste buds for these tastes using a separate teaspoon for each taste. Use the letters SA for salty, SO for sour, and BI for bitter. Remember to rinse your mouth between each taste.

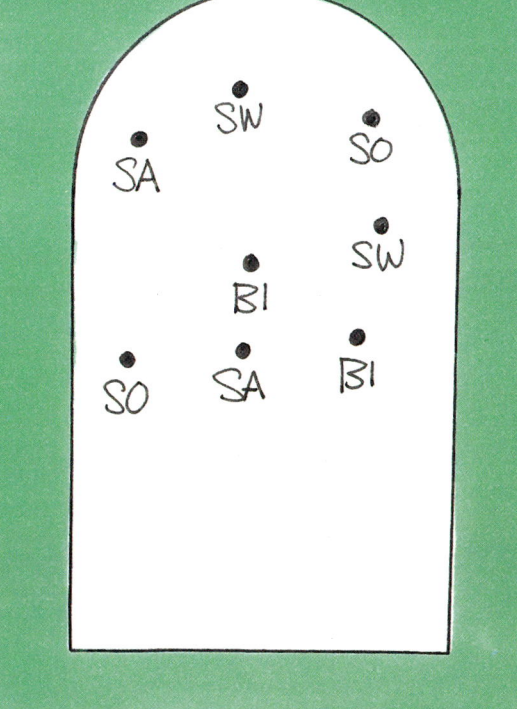

6 Begin again with sugar. This time, dip the tip of the spoon into the solution and place it on any part of your tongue. Let any liquid on the spoon run off on to your tongue.

13

Experiment with touch

The main organs of 'feeling' are nerve endings lying just below the surface of the skin. Some of these nerve endings sense heat and cold, some sense pain, and some sense touch. These nerve endings are not distributed evenly throughout the body, however, as you can discover by this experiment.

You Will Need
2 sharp pencils
Paper and pencil
A blindfold (a large handkerchief will do)
A friend

1 Blindfold yourself, or ask your friend to do it for you.

2 Ask your friend to press the point of one of the pencils lightly on the palm of your hand. Get him or her to repeat the action, this time using the points of two pencils held 5 millimetres apart. Let your friend continue to do this, sometimes using one and sometimes two pencil points. Say how many pencil points you think are pressing on your hand each time, and keep a record of how many times you get it right.

3 Now repeat the experiment, with your friend pressing the pencil points on the skin of your upper back, close to your spine. You won't be able to tell how many pencil points are being used this time. This is because there are more nerve endings on the skin of your hand than there are on your back. Try other parts of your body and see what results you get. Then try the same experiments on your friend.

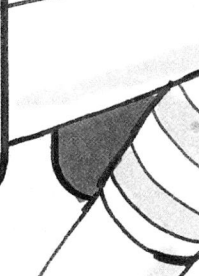

Test your lung capacity

You can increase the capacity of your lungs (the amount of air you can inhale in one breath) by regular exercise accompanied by deep breathing. Here is a simple way to measure your lung capacity. You can measure it before and after a physical fitness campaign to see if it changes.

You Will Need
A large bucket
A 5-litre (1 gallon) jar
Rubber tubing (about 1 m long)
Water

1 Put about 5 centimetres of water in the bucket.

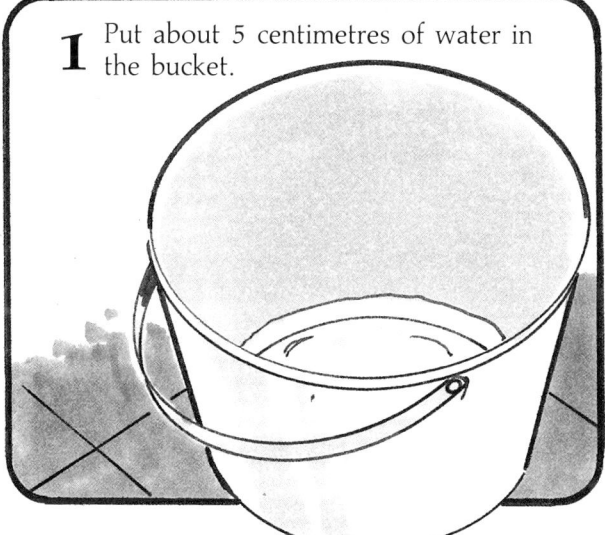

2 Fill the jar with water and quickly turn it upside down in the bucket so that the water stays in the jar.

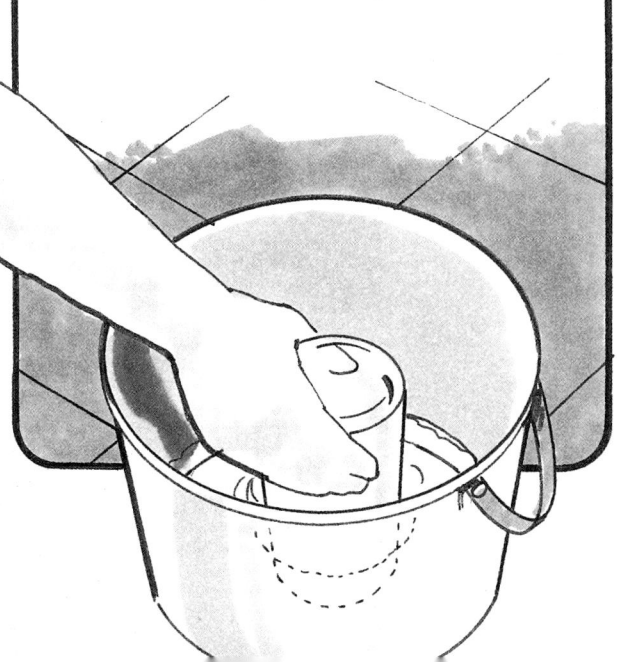

3 Tilt the jar slightly so that you can put one end of the rubber tubing into the mouth of the jar.

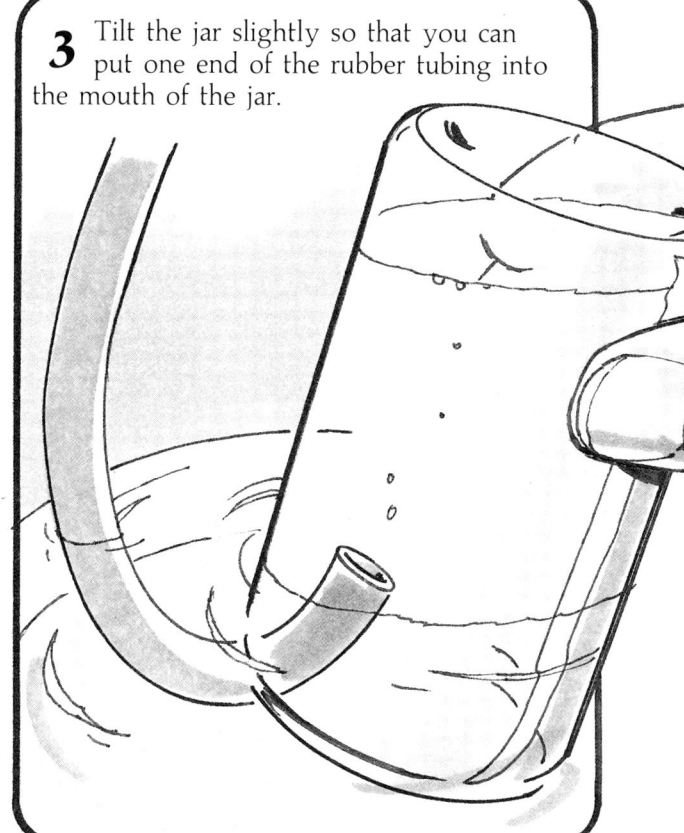

4 Inhale as deeply as you can and then blow into the outside end of the tube. See how much water you can force out of the jar into the bucket, with one breath. The more water you can force out, the larger your lung capacity.

15

Find your blind spot

Our eyes are the organs of sight. Light enters the pupil (which is a hole in the circular structure called the iris) and is focused on to the back of the eye (the retina) by the lens. The back of the eye is coated with nerve endings which are sensitive to light. The nerve endings connect with the optic nerve and carry the light images to the brain, where they are interpreted as shapes, giving us a picture of our surroundings. At the point at which the optic nerve enters the back of the eye there are no nerve endings. Here, any light falling on the retina is not registered by the brain. Thus this part of the retina is called the *blind spot*.

Here's how you can prove the existence of the blind spot.

You Will Need
This book

The Eye

retina

lens

central canal

iris

optic nerve

2 Close your left eye and hold the page before your right eye. Fix your gaze on the cross.

3 Now move the book towards you and then away from you. Suddenly you will find a point at which the dot disappears completely. This is because the light from the dot is focused on the blind spot and is not 'seen' by the brain.

1 Look at the cross and dot printed in this box.

See the fish in the bowl

If you look steadily at a light for a few seconds, then turn it off, you will still see the image of the light. This is because of a reaction of the eyes called *persistence of vision*. The retina of your eye retains the image of the object for a moment after the light is removed.

Before motion pictures were invented, people tried many ways of getting action in pictures using what they knew about persistence of vision. This experiment shows one method they used.

You Will Need
A piece of cardboard about 10 cm square
2 rubber bands
A felt-tip pen
A ruler
A friend

1 Draw a large picture of a fish on one side of the cardboard.

2 Turn the cardboard over, bottom to top, and draw a large picture of a fish bowl on the other side.

3 Punch a hole in each side of the card, exactly in the middle between top and bottom. (*Find the middle by measuring with a ruler.*)

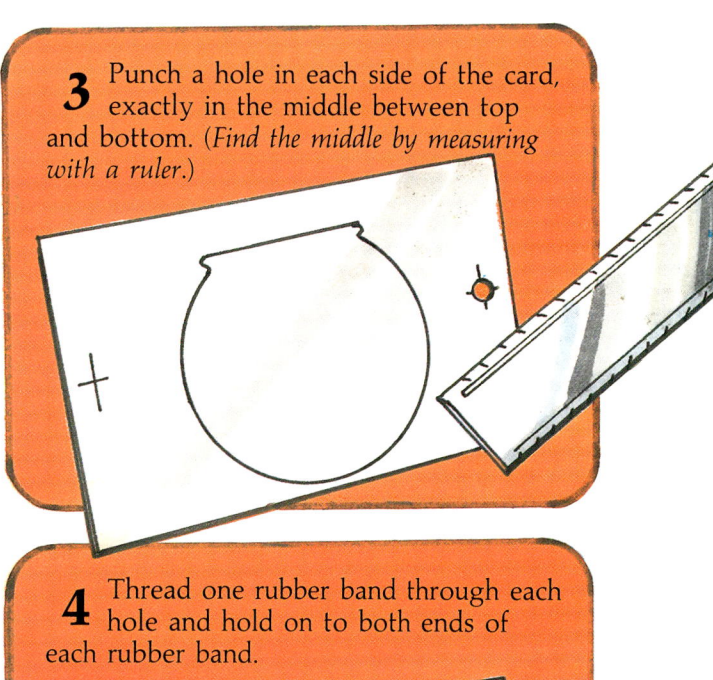

4 Thread one rubber band through each hole and hold on to both ends of each rubber band.

5 Ask your friend to 'wind up' the card as shown in the illustration, and then let go. The card will spin very fast. Watch it as it spins. It will look as if the fish is swimming in the bowl. This happens because the card spins so fast that you will seem to be seeing the fish and bowl at the same time due to persistence of vision.

☆ Make a simple microscope

A microscope is an instrument used for looking at tiny things. It has lenses which are pieces of glass of a special shape. If you look through them, at an object, they make it appear larger.

The first microscope was made by a Dutch wool merchant. For a lens, it simply used a piece of glass mounted on a metal frame which could be moved up and down for focus. You can easily make a microscope that can magnify as much as that first microscope, except that your microscope uses a drop of water for the lens instead of a piece of glass. A lens can be any clear substance that has a definite shape and will bend light rays as they pass through it.

You Will Need
3 tin cans (one can must be empty)
Shears
A hammer and nail
A small block of wood
Grease or cooking oil
A pencil
A small pane of glass
A small flat mirror
Sticky tape
An adult

1 Ask an adult to cut a strip of tin from the empty tin can using the shears. This strip should be about 3 centimetres wide and 10 centimetres long. Cover the edges with sticky tape so that you do not cut yourself afterwards.

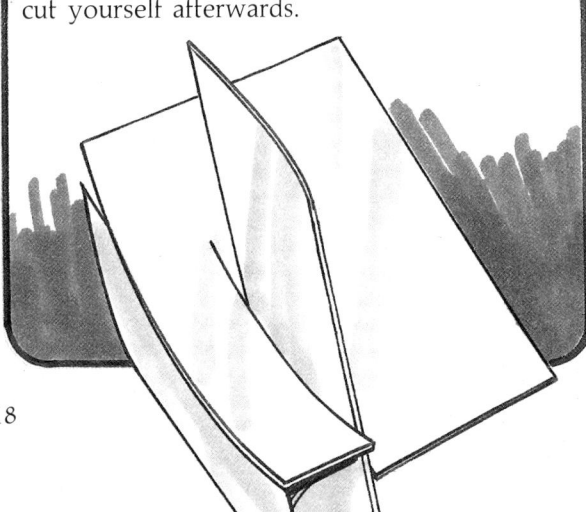

2 In the exact centre of the strip make a hole no more than 2 millimetres across. Ask an adult to do this by placing the strip on the piece of wood and driving the nail through it. Remove the nail from the hole.

3 Bend the ends of the strip downwards so that it will stand, and rub a little grease or oil around the hole.

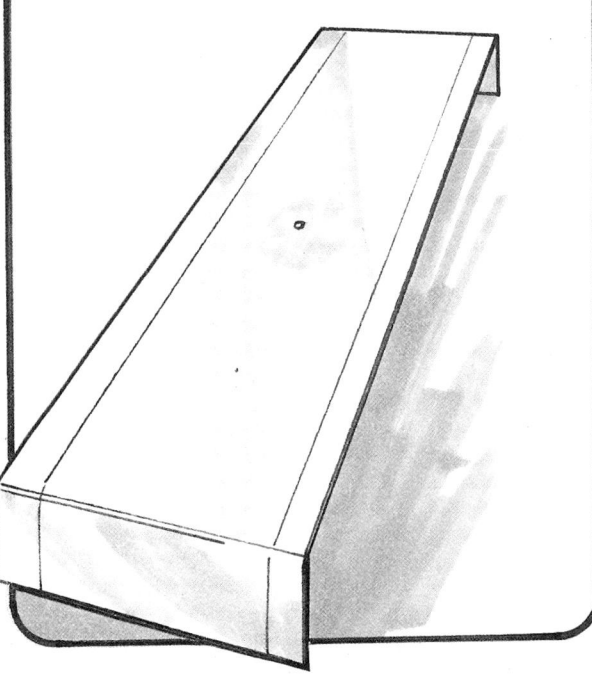

18

4 Dip the pencil in water and transfer a drop of water from the end of the pencil to the hole.

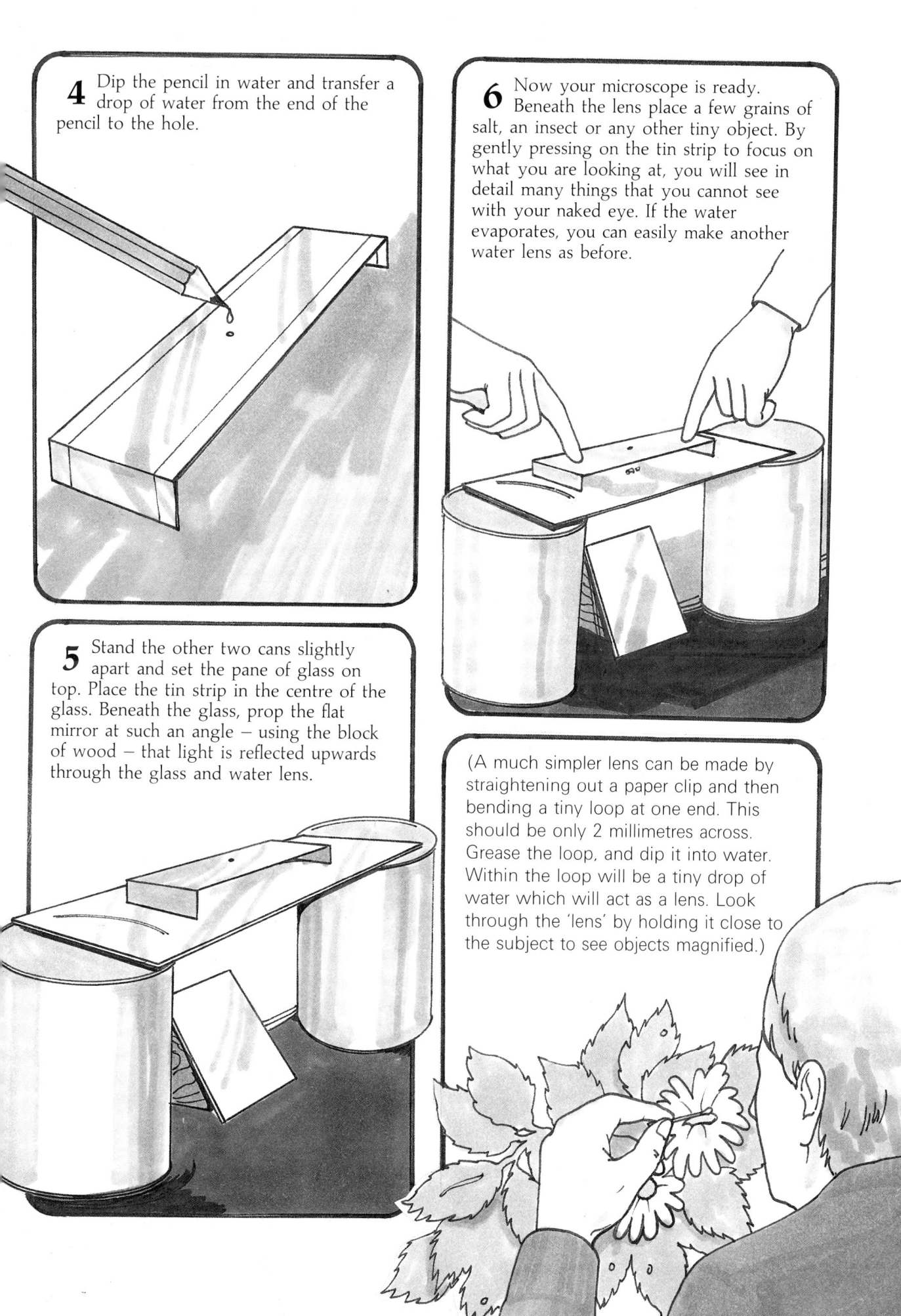

5 Stand the other two cans slightly apart and set the pane of glass on top. Place the tin strip in the centre of the glass. Beneath the glass, prop the flat mirror at such an angle — using the block of wood — that light is reflected upwards through the glass and water lens.

6 Now your microscope is ready. Beneath the lens place a few grains of salt, an insect or any other tiny object. By gently pressing on the tin strip to focus on what you are looking at, you will see in detail many things that you cannot see with your naked eye. If the water evaporates, you can easily make another water lens as before.

(A much simpler lens can be made by straightening out a paper clip and then bending a tiny loop at one end. This should be only 2 millimetres across. Grease the loop, and dip it into water. Within the loop will be a tiny drop of water which will act as a lens. Look through the 'lens' by holding it close to the subject to see objects magnified.)

Are your eyes deceiving you?

Optical illusions are caused by several things. Sometimes our eyes do not look properly at the object and give misleading information to the brain. Sometimes the brain has never had to try to sort out the kind of pictures it receives when it is confronted by optical illusions, and therefore has no experience of them on which to call. How do you get on with the following illusions?

Is this hat taller than it is wide?

Are the blue surfaces the bottom or the top of the cubes?

Is the centre piece the top or the bottom of the box?

Does this pattern move?

Can you see two heads or a candlestick?

The Muller-Leyer illusion. Which line is longer?

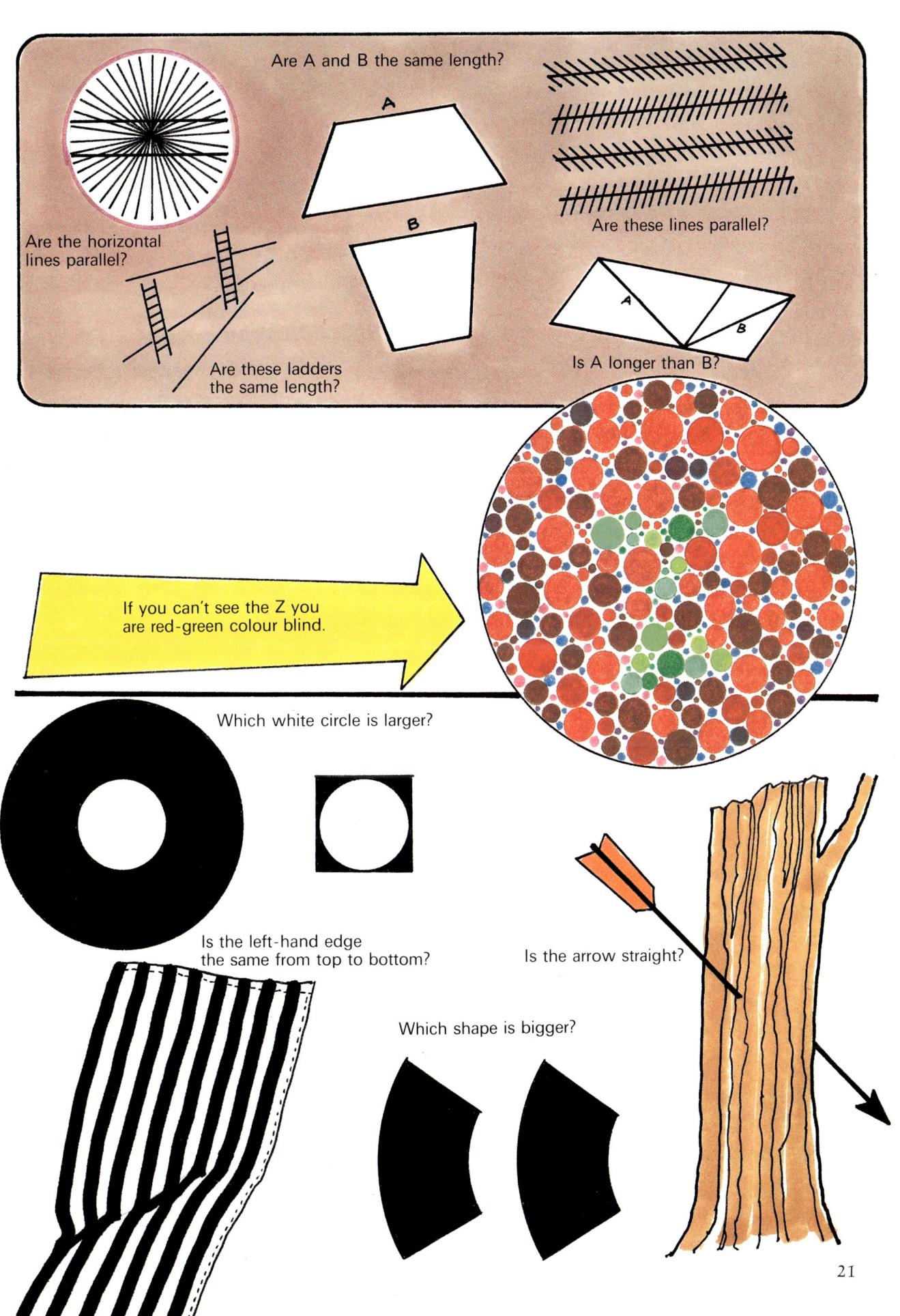

Are A and B the same length?

Are the horizontal lines parallel?

Are these lines parallel?

Are these ladders the same length?

Is A longer than B?

If you can't see the Z you are red-green colour blind.

Which white circle is larger?

Is the left-hand edge the same from top to bottom?

Is the arrow straight?

Which shape is bigger?

Make a periscope

You can make a periscope just like the ones submarine commanders use to see what's above the waves. You can use it for looking over walls or around corners. Following these instructions will result in a lot of fun.

You Will Need
2 small cardboard boxes
2 small mirrors
A knife or scissors
Sticky tape

1 Cut the tops and bottoms off both boxes.

2 Cut a hole in one side of each box, as shown below.

3 Tape a mirror into each box so that you can see it through the hole you have just made. Try to tape the mirrors at about 45°, as shown.

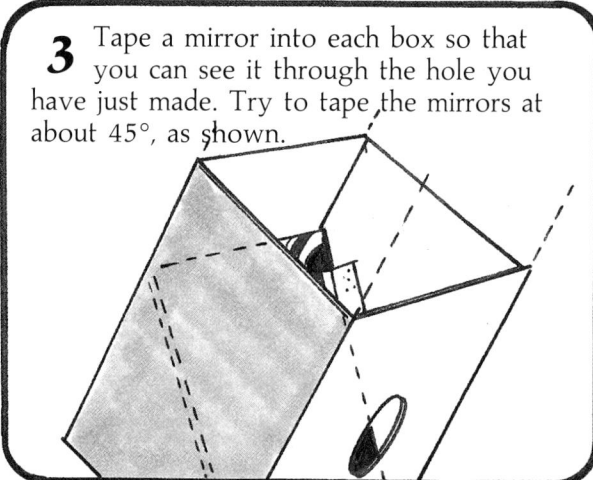

4 Now fit the two boxes one inside the other so that the two holes are on opposite sides. Tape the boxes together.

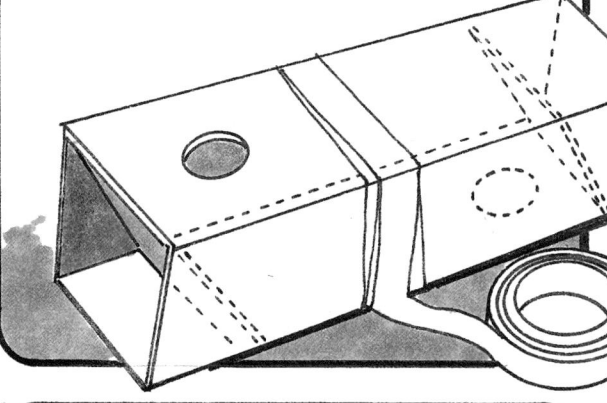

5 Your periscope is now ready for use. Try looking over a wall or around a corner. Look through one hole while the other hole is above the wall. Because light travels in straight lines, and is reflected by the mirrors, you will be able to see objects even though you are out of sight and cannot see them directly.

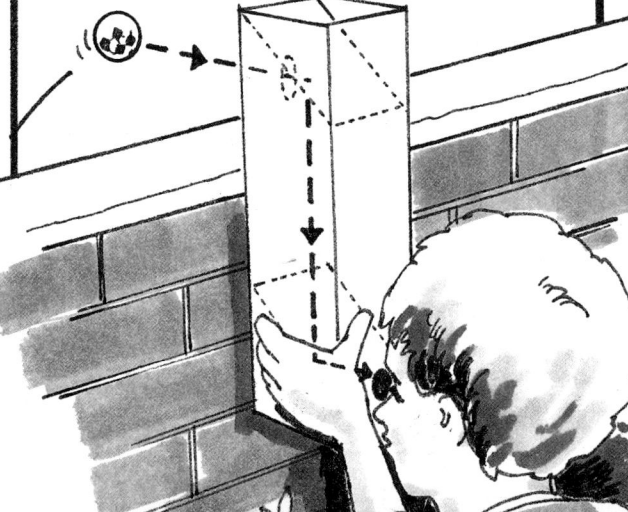

☆ What are bones made of?

About two-thirds of the tissue which makes up a bone is composed of hard minerals such as calcium phosphate. The other third is soft matter. By treating bones in various ways we can remove either the hard or the soft matter.

You Will Need
Leg bones from a chicken
Vinegar
A large tin
A jam jar
An adult

Cross-section of a bone

Heat one bone in the tin for an hour. Ask an adult to put it in the oven for you. The soft matter will be destroyed, and the bone will be whitish and brittle. The ash will consist of mineral compounds.

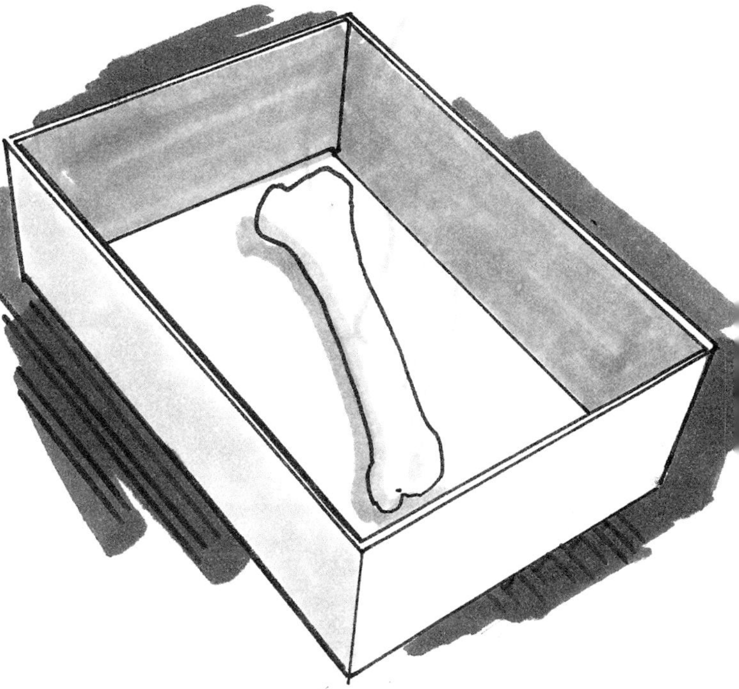

Drop another bone into the jam jar, containing undiluted vinegar, and leave it for a few days. Remove the bone and rinse it thoroughly. Notice that the bone is no longer stiff. You can bend it. The mineral matter has been dissolved away by the vinegar leaving only the animal matter.

Test your reflexes

Some of our actions are planned in advance – deciding to pick up a pencil, for instance. But many are under the control of a sort of 'automatic pilot'. Even when our brain is asleep we carry on breathing, for instance.

Here are some reflex actions for you to try.

You Will Need
A friend
A mirror
A feather (or any object to tickle with)

1 Ask your friend to make a quick movement in front of your eyes. Try not to blink.

2 Ask your friend to tickle the back of your neck with a feather. Can you avoid goose pimples on your skin?

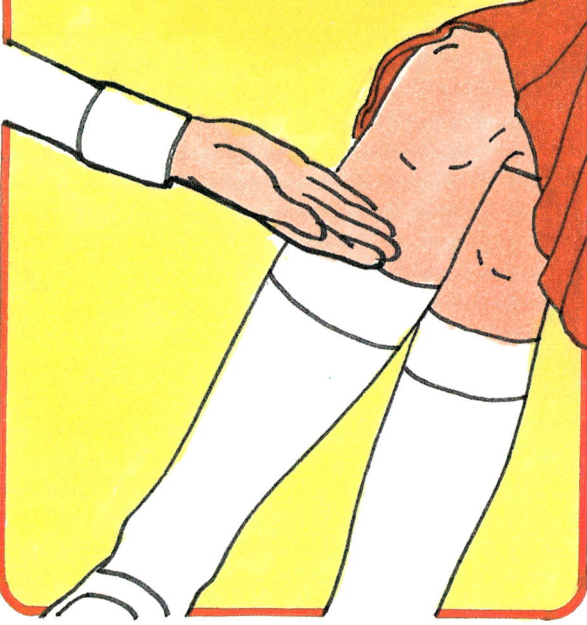

3 Sit relaxed on a chair and cross your legs. Ask your friend to tap with the side of the hand just below your knee when you are not watching. Can you stop your foot from kicking out?

4 Place the mirror in front of a window during daylight. Stand in front of the mirror. Cover one eye for about five seconds. Now take your hand away quickly and watch the pupil (the small dark area in the centre of the eye) suddenly grow smaller. In dark conditions it expands to allow maximum light to enter the eye, but in bright light it automatically closes so that not too much light enters the eye.

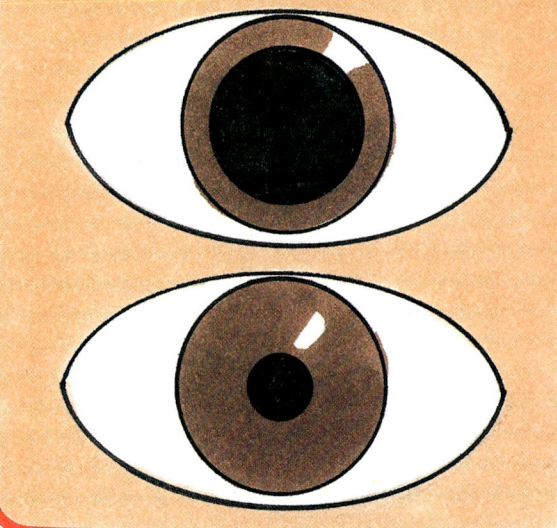

How quick are your reactions?

Your reaction time varies from day to day, and depends on whether or not you are tired, your age and many other factors.

Here's a simple way to see how fast the reactions of you and your friends are.

You Will Need
A piece of paper about 13 cm × 7 cm
A friend

Ask your friend to hold out a hand with the thumb and forefinger about 2 centimetres apart. Suspend the piece of paper between your friend's thumb and forefinger with your own hand. Then, without giving any warning, let go of the paper. Your friend must try to catch it, only by closing thumb and forefinger when the paper drops. Try it the other way round, with your friend holding the paper. You can also try it at different times of the day to see if your reaction time varies.

NAME	Morning	Midday	Afternoon	Evening
Fred	0	1	1	0
Nan	1	2	3	0
Mum	2	3	1	2
Dad	2	1		
Nancy	2	1		
David	3	0	2	1
Sally	2	3	4	0

Test other friends and your family, and make a record of their reaction times. See, for instance, how many times out of 10 they can catch the paper, or at what time of day their reactions are best.

Is ice lighter than water?

If you were asked which was heavier, a bucket of ice or a bucket of water, you would probably say the ice was heavier, because solids seem heavier than liquids. You'd be wrong in this case, though, for ice is in fact lighter, or less dense, than water.

Here is a way to demonstrate the fact that ice is lighter than water.

You Will Need
An empty tin can
A ruler
Water
The freezer compartment of a refrigerator

2 Place the tin and its water in the freezer compartment of a refrigerator.

3 When it has frozen solid, measure the space between the top of the ice and the top of the tin. You will find that the space is much less with the ice. Leave the ice to thaw out, and you will find that the water occupies the same volume it did before you froze it.

The water expanded as it froze becoming less dense. Less dense objects float on denser ones, which is why ice floats on water. If you topped up the water to the same level that the ice was at, the tin would weigh more. Therefore a tin of ice must weigh less than a tin with the same level of water.

1 Half fill the tin with cold tap water and carefully measure the space between the surface of the water and the top of the tin.

Will things dissolve faster in hot or cold water?

You Will Need
2 cups exactly the same size
2 teaspoons
Hot water
Cold water
Salt or sugar

1 Fill the cups with equal amounts of water. The water in one cup should be very hot, and the water in the other cup should be very cold.

2 Add *either* a teaspoonful of salt, *or* a teaspoonful of sugar to both of them. Stir them both equally and see which one dissolves first.

The teaspoonful which went into the hot water dissolved first because the hot water made the molecules move faster and speeded up the dissolving process.

Molecules are small groups of atoms, which are the smallest particles of any substance. Atoms are very small, so small that there are about a million in the thickness of a piece of paper. However there are only about one hundred different types of atoms. Some things are made of atoms that are all the same, such as the gases hydrogen and oxygen, and metals like gold and silver. Everything else is made of a combination of different atoms. Water, for example, is made of hydrogen and oxygen atoms, whereas sugar has carbon, hydrogen and oxygen atoms. A hydrogen atom from sugar is exactly the same as a hydrogen atom from water.

Atoms attract each other and can grip each other very tightly. In most things the atoms form molecules which do not grip one another as tightly as atoms do. In liquids and gases the molecules are free, which is why they flow easily and absorb or dissolve other substances.

27

☆ Make a rocket-propelled boat

You Will Need

A lid of a large soap dish (or bottom of an old tobacco or other flat tin)

Wire

A candle

A small tin with a tight-fitting, preferably screwcap, lid (the sort of tin in which talcum powder is often sold is ideal)

A hammer and nail

Water

An adult

1 Ask an adult to punch a small hole in the bottom of the tin with the hammer and nail. *Check to see that the hole goes right through.*

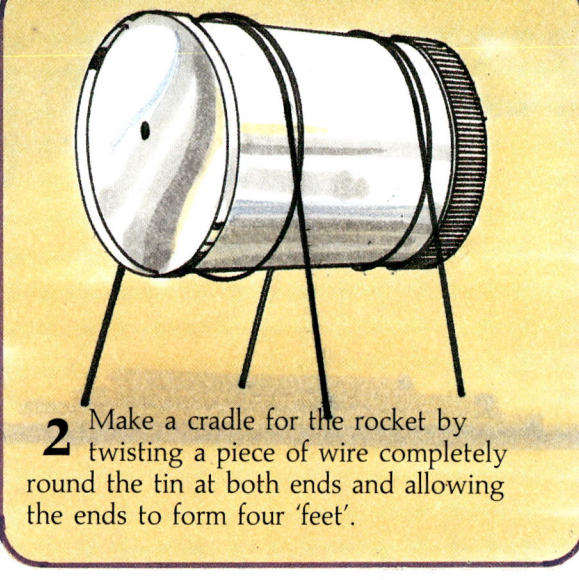

2 Make a cradle for the rocket by twisting a piece of wire completely round the tin at both ends and allowing the ends to form four 'feet'.

3 Get an adult to secure the candle in the lid of the soap dish and position the feet of the rocket in the corners of the lid. There must be sufficient room for the candle and its flame underneath the tin.

4 Half fill the rocket with water. Replace the cap and reposition the feet of the rocket in the corners of the lid of the soap dish so that the rocket is steady.

5 Float the dish in a bath or tub of water. Ask an adult to light the candle and watch what happens. Do not touch the rocket while it is hot.

As the water starts to boil, steam will build up and suddenly the rocket will shoot across the water as steam spurts out of the hole. The reason this happens is because the escape of steam, known as an action, causes a movement in the opposite direction. The opposite movement is called a reaction, and takes the form of the rocket speeding across the surface of the water.

☆ Make a water wheel

Water power used to be the main way to run machinery. Even today, hydroelectric schemes still use waterwheels built into dams to generate electricity. These wheels are called *turbines.* You can make a working water wheel which operates on exactly the same principle. Do this on a draining board.

You Will Need
A knitting needle
6 dip-pen nibs
A piece of wire (an old wire coat-hanger will do)
A cork
A tin can or plastic bottle
An empty jar
An adult

3 Twist the wire into the shape shown, and place the knitting needle in the cradle formed by the twisted wire. The needle should revolve freely. You have now made the turbine.

1 Push the knitting needle through the centre of the cork.

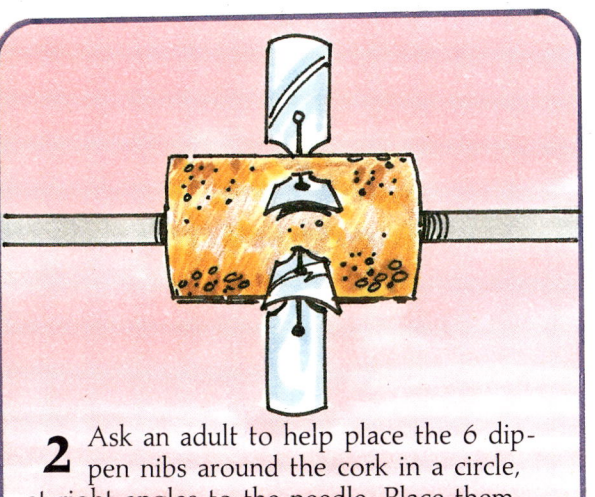

2 Ask an adult to help place the 6 dip-pen nibs around the cork in a circle, at right angles to the needle. Place them an equal distance from each other.

4 Punch a small hole in the side of the can or bottle. Place the can or bottle on the jar, to give it height, and fill it with water. As the water spurts from the hole you have made, position the turbine so that the water strikes the 'blades' and causes the turbine to revolve.

Does surface area affect evaporation?

Evaporation is the change of a liquid to a vapour, when molecules are lost from the surface. This happens at temperatures below as well as at boiling point.

Here is a way to find out how surface area affects evaporation.

You Will Need
A shallow saucer
A tumbler
A tablespoon
Water

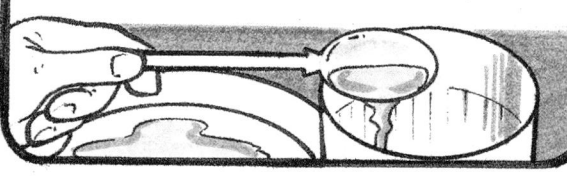

1 Put exactly a tablespoonful of water into both the shallow saucer and the tumbler.

2 Place both containers in a warm sunny place — on a windowsill or in the garden.

3 Check from time to time to see which is evaporating fastest.

The water in the saucer evaporates faster. It has a much greater surface area in contact with the air than the water in the tumbler, thus more molecules of water are lost from its surface in any given period of time. Eventually, all the water evaporates.

Will a needle float on water?

You Will Need
A sewing needle
A bowl of water

1 Lay the needle very gently on the surface of the water in a bowl. If you are careful, you will make it float. Look at the surface of the water from the side and see where it bends beneath the needle. The needle does not sink because water has a kind of 'skin' called *surface tension*. Certain insects use this skin to walk about on the surface of ponds.

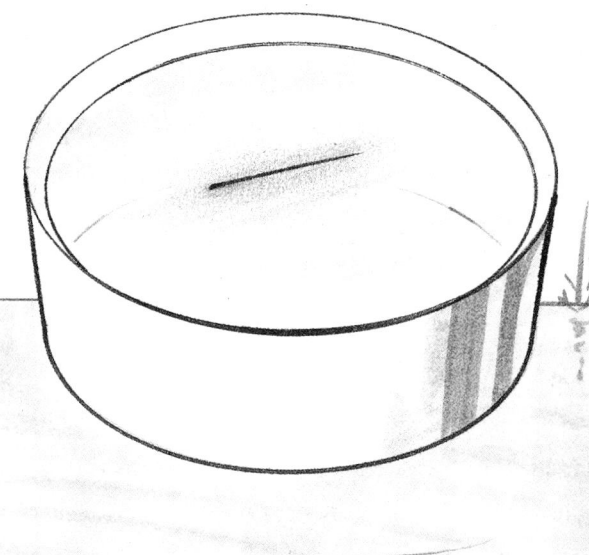

Surface tension exists because the water molecules pull one another, and the ones at the surface are pulled closer than those below the surface. The stronger pull between molecules at the surface is sufficient to prevent the needle sinking.

Study surface tension

The surface of water, or any other liquid, is in a state of tension, as if it were being pulled taut. In water, this causes the surface to be a little higher at the sides of a glass than in the centre. Here is another experiment to do with surface tension.

You Will Need
A basin
Water
2 wooden toothpicks or cocktail sticks
A little detergent or soap powder

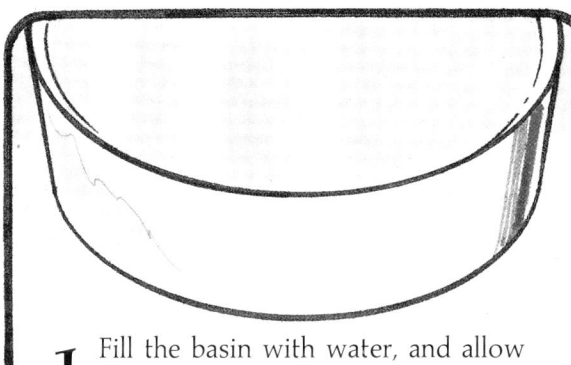

1 Fill the basin with water, and allow the water to settle.

3 Add a few grains of soap powder or detergent to the water. Gently stir the water. The detergent has the effect of reducing the surface tension of the water.

2 Place the toothpicks about 5 millimetres apart, side by side on the surface of the water, and watch what happens. The toothpicks will slowly move together. It is as though you had placed two broom handles near the middle of a rug which was being held taut by its edges. The broom handles would roll together.

4 Place the toothpicks on the surface of the water again, and watch what happens. The toothpicks will no longer be drawn towards each other.

Can water climb?

There are three experiments to do here.

You Will Need

2 or 3 narrow, clear tubes of differing thicknesses (Drinking straws of different widths, or straight pieces of plastic tubing will do.)

Water in a jar or cup

Vaseline

A test tube (A narrow round bottle wide enough to push your finger inside will do if you haven't got a test tube.)

The first experiment shows how water rises up tubes of differing thicknesses.

Place the jar or cup containing water on a table. Place the tubes in the water. Notice that the water rises highest in the narrowest tube, and least high in the widest tube.

The second experiment shows why water climbs up the tubes

Half fill the test tube with water. Look at the surface of the water. The sides seem to curve upwards. This curved shape is called a *meniscus*. The sides curve upwards because some of the water is attracted to the glass by *adhesion*.

Adhesion is what pulls the water up the tubes, and this pulling up is known as capillary action. Capillary action is strongest in the narrowest tube because most of the water in the tube is touching the sides and therefore attracted by adhesion.

The third experiment shows when water will not climb.

Grease the sides of the test tube with vaseline. Half fill it with water again, and look at the meniscus. It is curving down, instead of up. This is because the water molecules are not as strongly attracted to vaseline as they are to glass. The downward-curving meniscus is formed because the water molecules are more strongly attracted to each other than the vaseline, not by adhesion in this case, but by *cohesion*.

☆ Why are dams thicker at the bottom than at the top?

Did you know that a dam is built thicker at the bottom than at the top? This experiment will show you why.

You Will Need
A large tin can
A hammer and nail
Water
An adult

1 Ask an adult to punch three holes in the side of the can, using the hammer and nail; one near the top, one in the middle and one near the bottom.

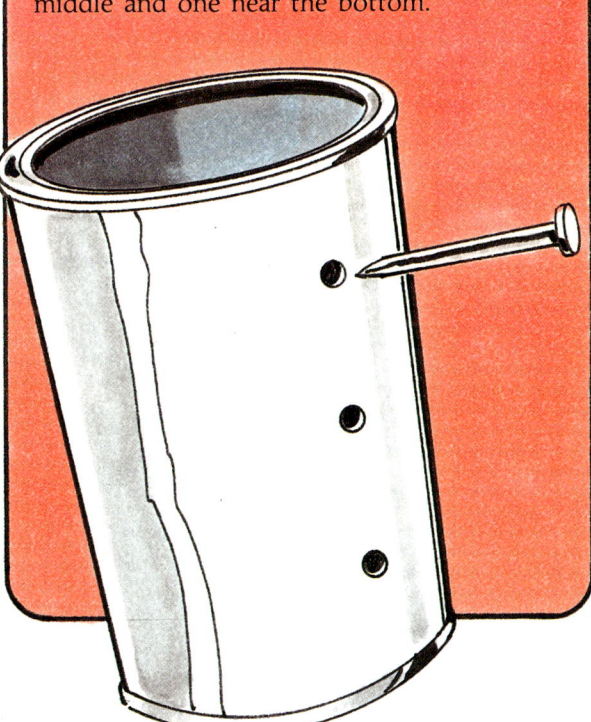

2 Turn the can upright on a draining board or in the garden and fill it with water. Watch the jets of water which spurt out from each of the holes. The jet of water from the bottom hole will spurt furthest. This is because the water pressure is greatest here, for here the water is deepest.

Dams are thicker at the base than at the top to withstand the greater pressures in the deeper water. The pressure is much less at the top so dams do not need to be as strong there.

Can water stretch?

You Will Need
A glass
Paper clips
Water

1 Fill the glass with water, right to the very top.

2 Carefully start to put paper clips into the water, end on, and see how many you can put in before water spills over the top of the glass.

You may have thought you could only get about 10 paper clips into the glass of water before the water started spilling over the top. You may even have thought that since the glass was already full, anything at all placed into it would have caused the water to spill over. But it is amazing how many paper clips you can get in.

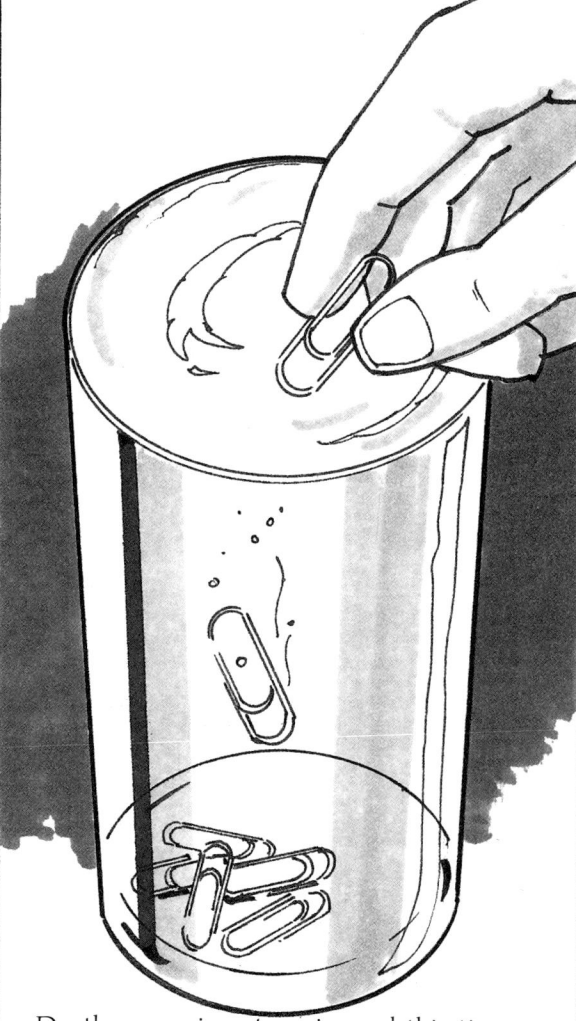

Do the experiment again, and this time, as you add paper clips, look, from the side, at what is happening to the surface of the water. It is rising and 'stretching'. This is because the surface tension of water will allow it to bulge as you add the paper clips. (See also pages 30–31.)

Make a hydrometer

A *hydrometer* is an instrument used to measure the specific gravity, or relative weight, of a liquid. To find the specific gravity of a liquid, its density is compared to the density of water. A real hydrometer is constructed with a hollow glass float which is weighted at the bottom so that it stands upright in the liquid. When the hydrometer is put in a liquid, the glass float sinks until it displaces its own weight of liquid. The specific gravity of the liquid can then be read on a scale which is in the hydrometer.

Here's how to make your own hydrometer. It will not tell you the specific gravity of a liquid, but it will tell you whether the liquid is heavier (denser) or lighter (less dense) than water. It will not sink as deeply in a denser liquid as it does in water.

You Will Need

A drinking glass or jam jar
A plastic lipstick top
Small screws
Masking tape
Sugar
Milk
Water

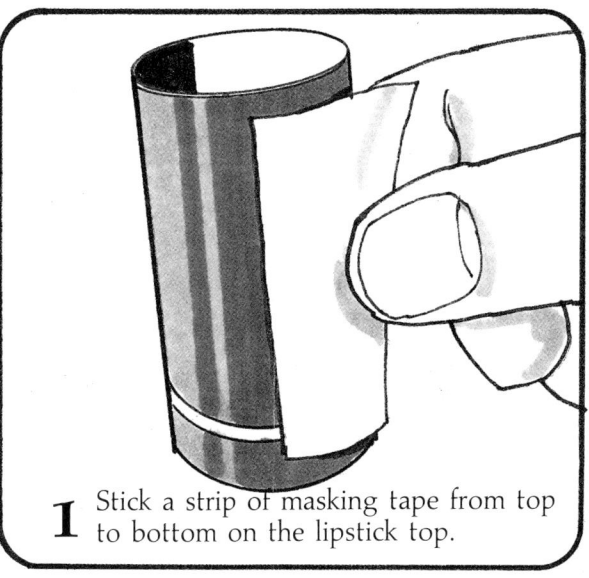

1 Stick a strip of masking tape from top to bottom on the lipstick top.

2 Place seven or eight small screws in the top. Test it to see whether it floats upright in a glass of water. If it sinks, take out some of the screws. If it tips, shake the screws around until it balances. Mark the water level on the tape.

3 Dissolve a quarter of a cup of sugar in the water and put the top and screws in the water without changing the number of screws. See whether the water level, and therefore the specific gravity of the solution, is different to that of water.

If the specific gravity is higher, the liquid is denser and the tube floats higher than it does in water since it has to displace less liquid to equal its weight. The water level will be lower on your hydrometer. Test milk, syrup, water with salt in and other liquids.

☆ Make water rise

You Will Need
A shallow dish
A candle
Water
A jam jar
An adult

1 Ask an adult to light the candle and to drip some wax from the candle into the dish for the candle to stand in securely.

2 Carefully pour some water around the candle in the dish. If the candle goes out, relight it.

3 Once the candle is burning, place the jam jar over the candle in the dish. The candle will burn for a while and then go out. Watch what happens to the water.

The water rose up inside the jar. This happened because the candle used up the air in the jar. (It needed the oxygen in the air to stay alight.) When the air was used up, there was a vacuum, and water was sucked in to fill the vacuum. Before the candle used up the air and then went out, the air in the jam jar was keeping the water out.

Does rust make water rise?

You Will Need
A large test tube or similar glass vessel
Iron filings or steel wool
Water
A dish

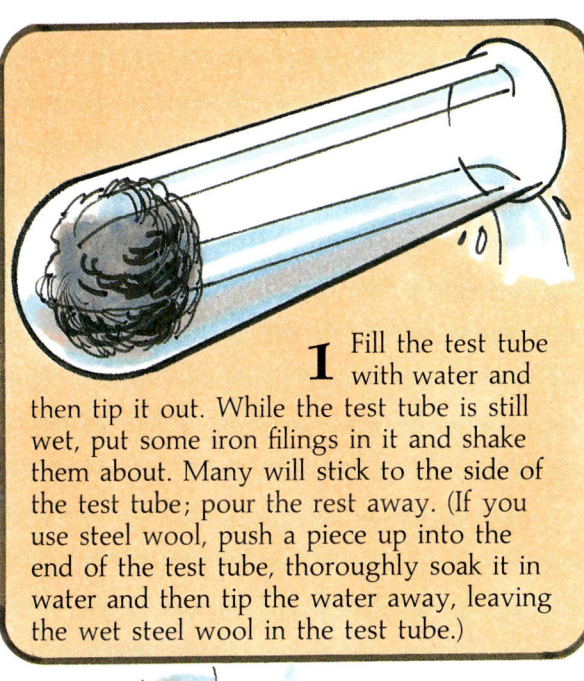

1 Fill the test tube with water and then tip it out. While the test tube is still wet, put some iron filings in it and shake them about. Many will stick to the side of the test tube; pour the rest away. (If you use steel wool, push a piece up into the end of the test tube, thoroughly soak it in water and then tip the water away, leaving the wet steel wool in the test tube.)

2 Turn the test tube upside down and stand it in a dish containing about 2 centimetres of water.

3 Look at the test tube the next day and note what has happened. Some of the water has risen up the inside of the test tube, which means some of the air has been used up, and water has risen to replace it. (See page 36).

The reason the air had been used up was because the iron filings had gone rusty. Rusting is a kind of burning process, and it therefore uses up oxygen from the air. The loss of air caused a vacuum, which the water filled.

Study currents in water

You Will Need
2 glass jars (the necks must be exactly the same size)
Ink or food colouring
Cardboard
Hot and cold water

1 Fill two jars, one with hot water and one with cold water. Put a few drops of food colouring in the hot water (in order to detect the movement of currents).

2 Hold a piece of cardboard over the mouth of the cold water jar and turn it upside down over the other jar.

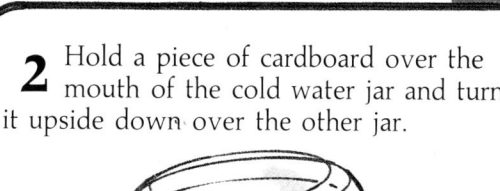

3 Carefully slide the cardboard out from between the jars, keeping the necks of the jars held closely to one another. Watch the action of the water in both jars.

The coloured hot water rose up into the other jar. This happened because the cold water is heavier than hot water. It descended into the lower bottle pushing the hot water up in small currents.

Does air contain water?

You Will Need
A drinking glass
Water
Cubes of ice
Ink or food colouring

Half fill the glass with water dyed with ink. Put some ice in the water and dry the outside of the glass. Drops of colourless moisture (water) will condense from the air on to the cold sides of the glass, proving that air contains water. The fact that they are colourless proves they did not come from inside the glass.

☆ Does air travel in a straight line?

You Will Need
A milk bottle (or any bottle)
A candle (about two thirds as tall as the bottle)
A metal tray
An adult

1 Ask an adult to light the candle and drip wax on to the tray for the candle to stand in securely.

2 Place the milk bottle about 5 centimetres in front of the candle.

3 Blow quite hard on the bottle on the side away from the candle and watch what happens to the candle.

The candle goes out because the air goes round the bottle and comes together again near the flame, causing it to be blown out. From this you can see that air doesn't always travel in a straight line.

How does an aeroplane fly?

What makes an aeroplane stay in the air? You might say its powerful engines, but a glider, which does not have an engine, can stay in the air too. An aeroplane can stay in the air because of the shape of its wings. The shape is called an *aerofoil*, and when air travels over the wings, it must travel faster over the top of the wings than over the bottom if all the air is to reach the back of them at the same time. These different air-flow speeds cause the air over the top of the wings to exert less pressure than the air underneath. This results in the wings, and therefore the aeroplane, being forced up by the phenomenon known as *lift*. The engines are needed to ensure that the aeroplane moves fast enough through the air for lift to occur. Here is a simple way to demonstrate lift.

You Will Need
A pencil
A piece of paper about 30 cm × 5 cm
Non-toxic glue

Hold the piece of paper with the short end towards you and blow over the top of it. The paper will rise because, by blowing, you caused the air to move faster along the top of the paper than along the bottom, resulting in lift.

forward movement creates air current over wing

lift makes
aircraft fly

air resistance
and gravity slow
aircraft down

weight of aircraft
pulls it down

You can make a model of an aeroplane
wing. Glue the two ends of the paper
together so that you make the shape
shown. Push the pencil through the paper
and rest the paper on a table. Blow over
the paper at the thick edge and it will
again rise.

☆ Tricks with air pressure

We may not be able to see the air around us, but it exerts a pressure which can do some remarkable things. Here are two tricks you can do.

You Will Need
A milk bottle
A hard-boiled egg without its shell
Newspaper
A taper
A glass of water
A square of cardboard (large enough to cover the top of the glass)
An adult

How to put an egg in a milk bottle

1 Crumple the sheet of newspaper and drop it into the milk bottle.

2 Ask an adult to light the taper and insert it into the bottle so that the paper catches fire.

3 Place the bottle on a firm surface, and when the flame goes out, immediately place the hard-boiled egg in the opening of the bottle and watch what happens.

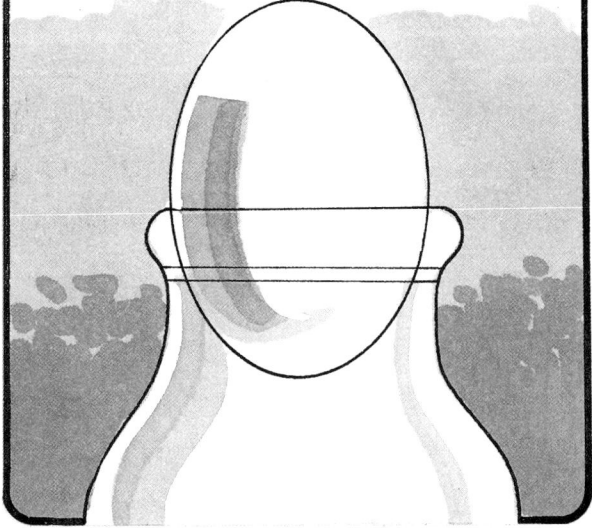

The egg was sucked into the bottle. This was because the burning paper used up all the air, so more air was sucked into the bottle to replace it. Anything else that was by the top of the bottle was sucked in too — even the hard-boiled egg!

How to turn a glass of water upside down without spilling the water

1 Fill the glass with water, to the top. Do this experiment over a sink.

2 Slide the cardboard over the top of the glass. If you have to push water away to get the cardboard on, so much the better.

3 Carefully turn the glass upside down and let go of the cardboard.

The water stays inside the glass because that invisible force called air pressure is holding the cardboard against the lip of the glass.

As you can see then, air pressure is very strong. The reason we do not feel the air pressing on our bodies is that the pressure is the same inside our lungs as it is on the outside of our bodies. In fact it is about the same as a force of 20 tonnes over the entire body.

As the experiment on page 44 shows, air pressure can be used to raise liquids. When you suck a drink through a straw your lungs work like a simple pump. Air pressure can lift water as much as 10 metres.

Air is also put to use by increasing its pressure with a compressor. Dentists' drills and the big drills used by road menders are powered by compressed air. Air pumped into an air bed or tyre is compressed to give enough force to support the weight of the person on the bed or the vehicle on the tyres. Hovercraft make dramatic use of air pressure by riding on a cushion of high-pressure air which enables them to travel over flat ground and water. This cushion is made by fans inside the hovercraft and is contained inside a flexible skirt.

Make water run uphill

You can use air pressure to make water run uphill, thus apparently defying the laws of gravity.

You Will Need
A rubber or plastic tube about 1 m long and 12 mm in diameter
2 buckets
Water

1 Fill one bucket three quarters full of water, and place it in a sink. Put the other bucket on the floor, below the first bucket.

2 Hold one end of the tube in each hand and fill the tube from the tap. Place your fingers over the ends of the tube to stop the water escaping.

3 Quickly place one end of the tube well below the surface of the water in the bucket in the sink. Keep your fingers over both ends still. Let the other end of the tube hang down above the bucket on the floor. This end must be lower than the end in the bucket in the sink.

4 Remove your fingers from both ends of the tube at the same time. Water will now flow uphill, from the top bucket, over its edge, and then down into the lower bucket. If the experiment does not work first time, refill the tube with water and try again. You must not let air enter the tube after you have filled it with water.

The water flowed uphill because as water fell out of the bottom end of the tube, air pressure on the surface of the water in the higher bucket pushed water into the tube to replace it. As water continued to fall out of the tube, more replaced it.

A tug of war with a vacuum

In 1654 a German scientist called Otto von Guericke demonstrated the force that could be exerted by air, or atmospheric, pressure. He carefully ground the rims of two metal hemispheres (you can imagine what a hemisphere looks like if you think of half a tennis ball), and then greased the rims. He then pushed the two metal hemispheres together, and removed the air using a special pump he had invented.

The air pressure was so great that it took two teams of eight horses − one team pulling on each hemisphere − to pull the hemispheres apart.

Here's how you can repeat von Guericke's experiment using rubber plungers.

You Will Need
2 plungers of the same size (the type used to clear blocked sinks)
A friend

1 Soak both plungers in water.

2 Ask a friend to sit on a chair and hold one plunger with its rubber cup facing upward.

3 Place the cup of the other plunger on to the one your friend is holding, and slowly and carefully push down until most of the air has been expelled from the plunger cups.

4 With each of you grasping a handle, see if you can pull the plungers apart. You'll be amazed how difficult it is.

You can still do this experiment even if you only have one plunger. Push it down on to a flat wet surface such as the bottom of a bucket containing a little water. Make sure you expel the air from inside the plunger, and then see how hard it is to pull it free.

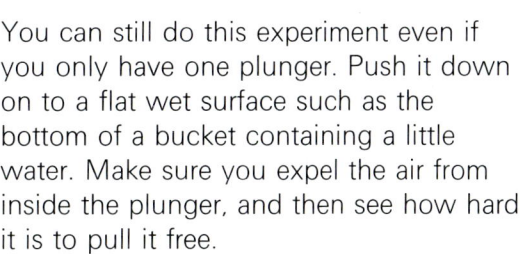

Does air have weight?

You Will Need
2 balloons
Thread
A pin
A stick about 1 m long

1 Tie a piece of thread to the middle of the piece of wood and hang the wood from a suitable structure so that it hangs free and horizontal, like the arms of a pair of scales.

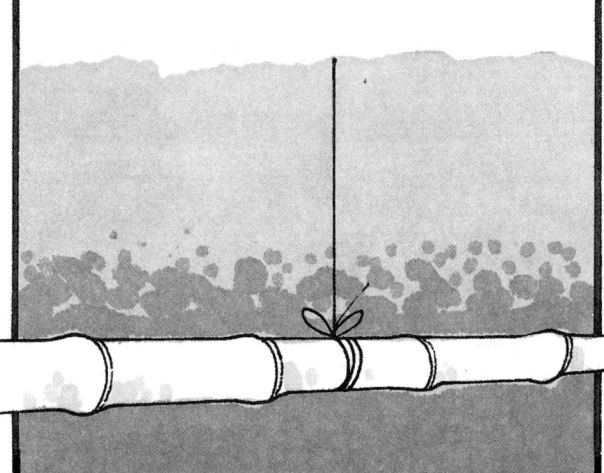

2 Blow up both the balloons so that they are approximately the same size, and tie each one up.

3 Tie a piece of thread about 45 centimetres long to each balloon. Make a loop in the end of each piece of thread, large enough to be slid freely along the piece of wood.

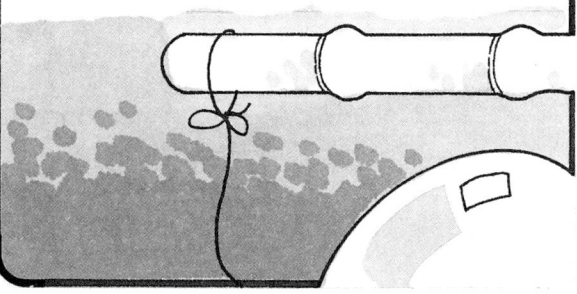

4 Hang a balloon on each end of the piece of wood. Adjust the position of the balloons by sliding them along the wood until the wood is balanced.

5 Allow the wood to become still, then burst one of the balloons with a pin and watch what happens.

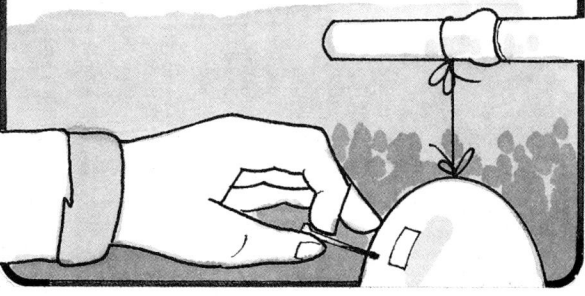

The unburst balloon will swing downwards, proving it is heavier than the burst balloon. Since the balloons themselves weigh the same (even though one is burst), the unburst balloon must be heavier because it still has air in it. The air therefore has weight.

A trick with air and water

Ask your friends whether they think you can place a handkerchief under water without getting it wet. They will probably laugh and say it is impossible, but here's how to do it.

You Will Need
A glass tumbler
A handkerchief
A bowl full of water

1 Push the handkerchief firmly into the bottom of the tumbler so that it occupies as little space as possible.

2 Turn the tumbler upside down and place it in the bowl of water, keeping the tumbler as straight as possible.

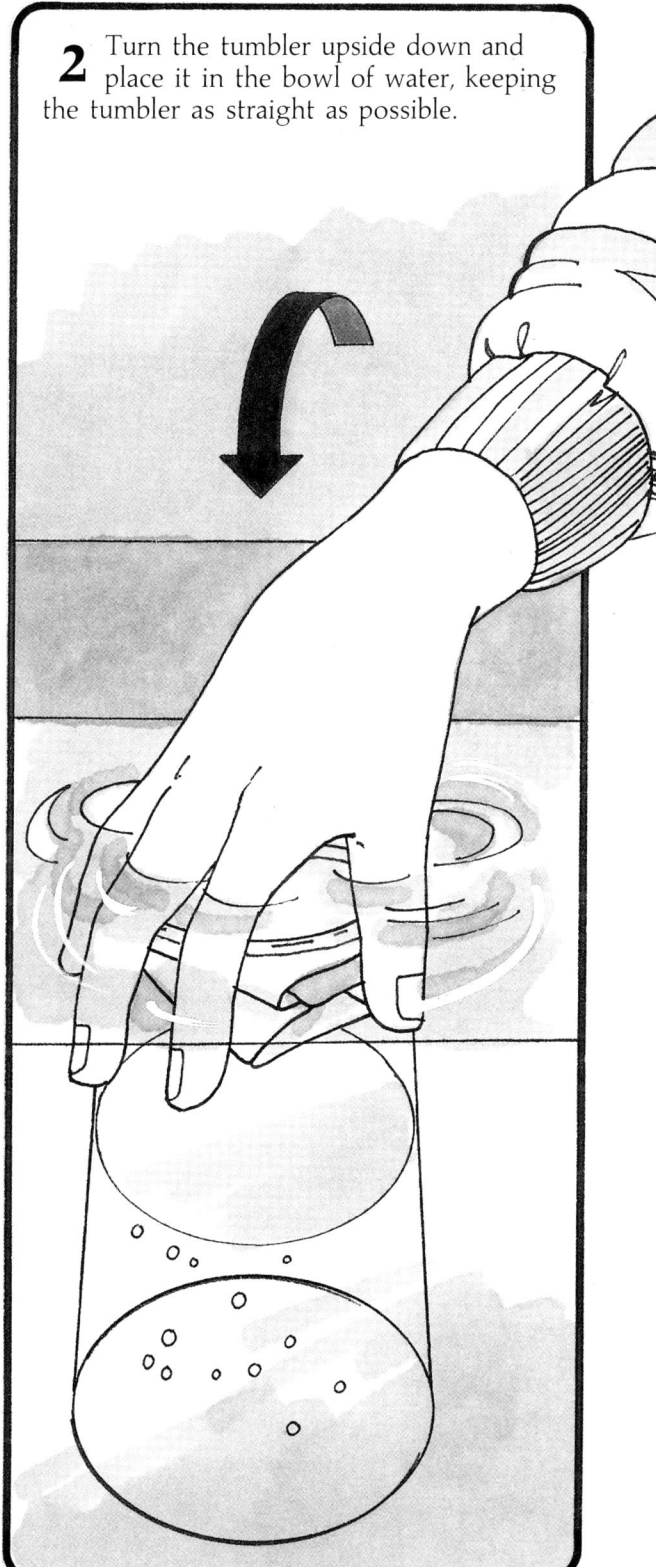

Although the water will rise a little way up the inside of the tumbler, the air inside the tumbler prevents it from rising all the way up, and so the handkerchief stays dry!

☆ A simple fire extinguisher

When something burns, it can only do so in the presence of oxygen. Oxygen is, of course, found in the air, too. One of the chemicals used to put out many types of fires is carbon dioxide, because it is heavier than air and thus pushes the air (and oxygen) away from the fire, so the fire goes out. Here is a way to demonstrate this.

You Will Need

An empty tin at least 12 cm high and big enough to hold three candles upright
3 candles of different heights (about 2.5 cm, 5 cm and 7.5 cm high)
1 tablespoonful of baking soda
2 tablespoonfuls of vinegar
An adult

1 Ask an adult to drip some melted wax on to the bottom of the tin and place the bases of unlit candles into the wax whilst it is still soft.

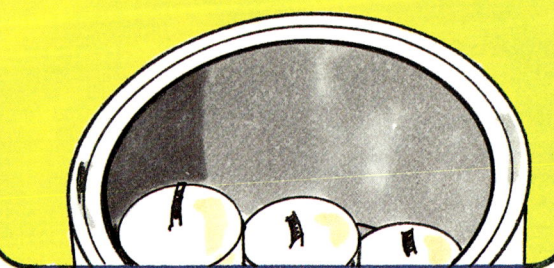

2 Sprinkle the baking soda in the bottom of the tin.

3 Ask an adult to light the candles.

4 When the candles are well lit, slowly pour the vinegar down the inside walls of the tin, being careful not to touch the flames and watch what happens. The vinegar and baking soda will react to produce carbon dioxide.

Bubbles of carbon dioxide will start to form in the bottom of the tin. As more carbon dioxide is produced it will rise, forcing the air out of the tin. When it reaches the level of the lowest candle flame, this will go out, followed by the next, and then the tallest, as the carbon dioxide reaches them, too, and pushes the oxygen away.

Performing moth balls

You Will Need
A drinking glass
A few moth balls
Baking soda
Vinegar

Fill the glass nearly full of water. Add a tablespoon of baking soda and stir until it is all dissolved. Then put a tablespoon of vinegar into the water. Drop about three moth balls into the solution and watch what happens.

Almost immediately, bubbles of gas will form on the moth balls, and the moth balls will float to the surface of the liquid. At the surface some of the bubbles will burst into the air. Then the moth ball to which they were attached will slowly sink. More bubbles will form on the moth ball and it will rise again. This will go on for some time, with moth balls rising and falling.

This happens because the mixture of vinegar and baking soda forms the gas carbon dioxide. Bubbles of this stick to the rough surface of the moth balls, and act as tiny floats.

49

Make stalactites and stalagmites

One of the features of caves in limestone areas is the beautiful formations called *stalactites* and *stalagmites*. They look like huge icicles, but are really calcium-salt deposits caused by constant drips of calcium-laden water coming from the ceiling of the caves. The water evaporates leaving stalactites to hang from the roof of the cave, and stalagmites which appear to grow from the ground.

You can cause similar deposits to occur, making your own stalactites and stalagmites.

You Will Need

A cardboard box (an old shoe box is ideal)
2 tall jars
Heavy string
2 nails
Epsom salts
Water

1 Place a tall jar on either side of the box. Leave the lid off the box.

2 Tie four pieces of heavy string to two nails. The strings must be long enough to reach from the bottom of one jar, over the top of the box, to the bottom of the other jar.

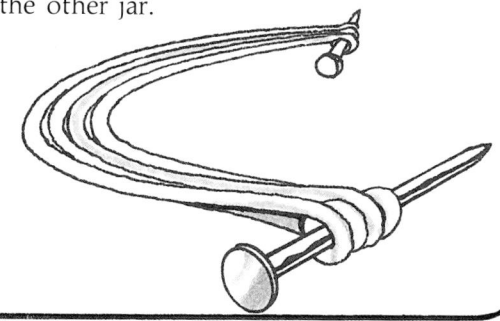

3 Make a saturated solution of Epsom salts by dissolving as much as you can in water. When no more will dissolve, the salts will just settle on the bottom of the jar.

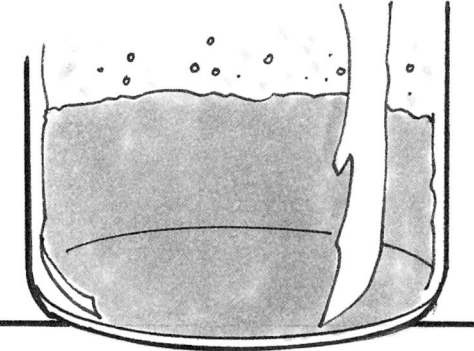

4 Fill each jar with the solution, and place a nail in each jar with the strings draped over the top of the box as shown. Soon the solution will start to creep up the strings. As it reaches the box, drips will fall into the bottom of the box. As the water evaporates from both the box and string, the salts that are left will gradually make stalactities and stalagmites.

Cut ice with pressure

Pressure causes heat. Because of this fact, you are able to skate on ice. The weight of your body, concentrated on the runners of your ice skates, causes the ice under the skates to melt due to the pressure. As the ice melts, the water produced acts as a lubricant allowing the skate to glide along. We can easily show how pressure can cause ice to melt by this experiment.

You Will Need

1 m of strong, narrow-gauge wire (strong fuse wire or wire similar to that inside plastic bag ties will do)
A block of wood
2 pencils
A cube of ice

1 Twist each end of the wire securely round the middles of the pencils. These will be the handles with which to hold on to the wire.

2 Place the cube of ice on top of the block of wood as shown, and place the middle of the wire across the middle of the cube.

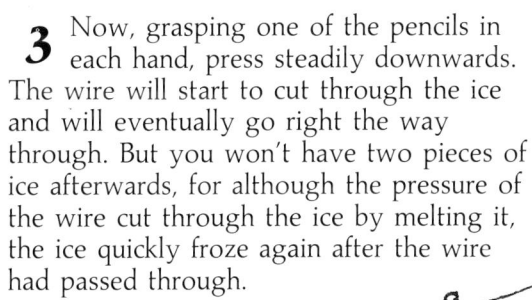

3 Now, grasping one of the pencils in each hand, press steadily downwards. The wire will start to cut through the ice and will eventually go right the way through. But you won't have two pieces of ice afterwards, for although the pressure of the wire cut through the ice by melting it, the ice quickly froze again after the wire had passed through.

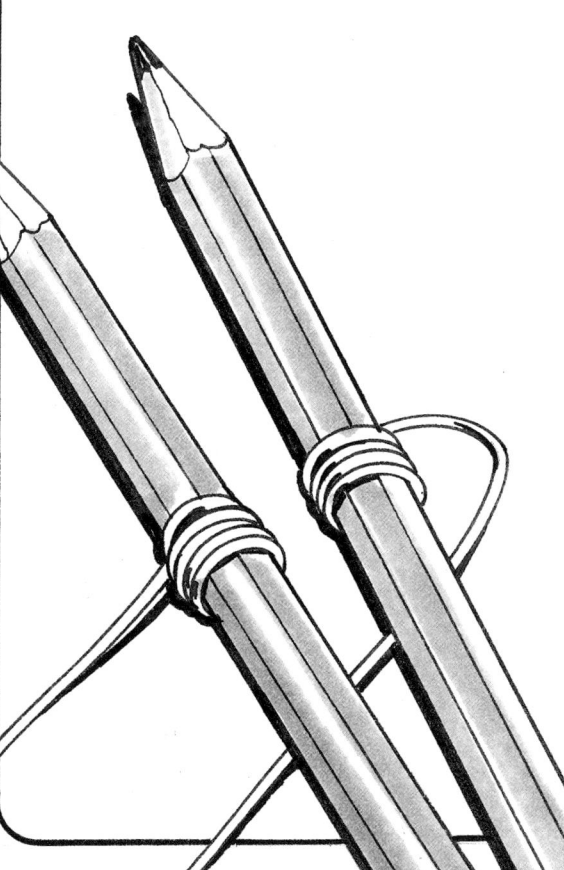

Which way is North?

Here are two compasses you can make.

Compass No 1
You Will Need
A saucer or shallow dish
Detergent (washing-up liquid will do)
Water
A magnet
A sewing needle
A slice of cork about 6 mm thick

2 Magnetize the needle. If you have a magnet with the two poles – north and south – clearly shown, magnetize your needle so that the pointed end is north, and the blunt end is south. Do this by stroking the needle from the middle towards the blunt end, using the north pole (end) of your magnet. Do this about 50 times, raising the magnet well clear of the needle after each stroke. Then stroke the needle from the middle towards the pointed end, using the south pole (end) of your magnet. Do this about 50 times. You have now magnetized the needle.

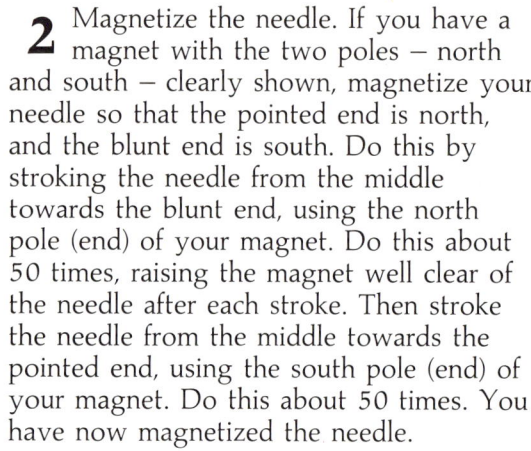

1 Place some water in the saucer and add a drop of detergent. The detergent will allow the cork to float freely.

3 If you do not have a magnet with the poles marked, then simply use one end of the magnet to magnetize one end of the needle, and the other end of the magnet to magnetize the other end of the needle. You will then have to borrow a compass to find out which end of your needle is north, and which end is south.

4 Push the needle through the middle of the cork, and float the cork on the water in the dish. It will turn so that the needle points north and south. In this picture the eye of the needle is north.

Compass No 2
You Will Need
A magnet
A sewing needle
Thread
A bottle, wider than the needle, and its cork
A drawing pin
A small piece of paper

1 Magnetize a needle as already described for Compass No 1.

2 Fold the paper to make a small cradle, and attach it to a short piece of thread. Attach the other end of the thread to the bottom of the cork from a bottle using the drawing pin.

3 Balance the magnetized needle in the cradle of paper and lower it into the bottle. Adjust the thread so that the needle hangs clear of the bottom of the bottle. Push the cork on to the bottle. The needle will swing round so that it faces in a north-south direction.

A trick with magnets

You can make a magnet float on air by using the laws of magnetism. Unlike poles attract, like poles repel.

You Will Need
2 bar magnets or 2 horseshoe magnets
A small cardboard box
6 ice lolly sticks or pencils

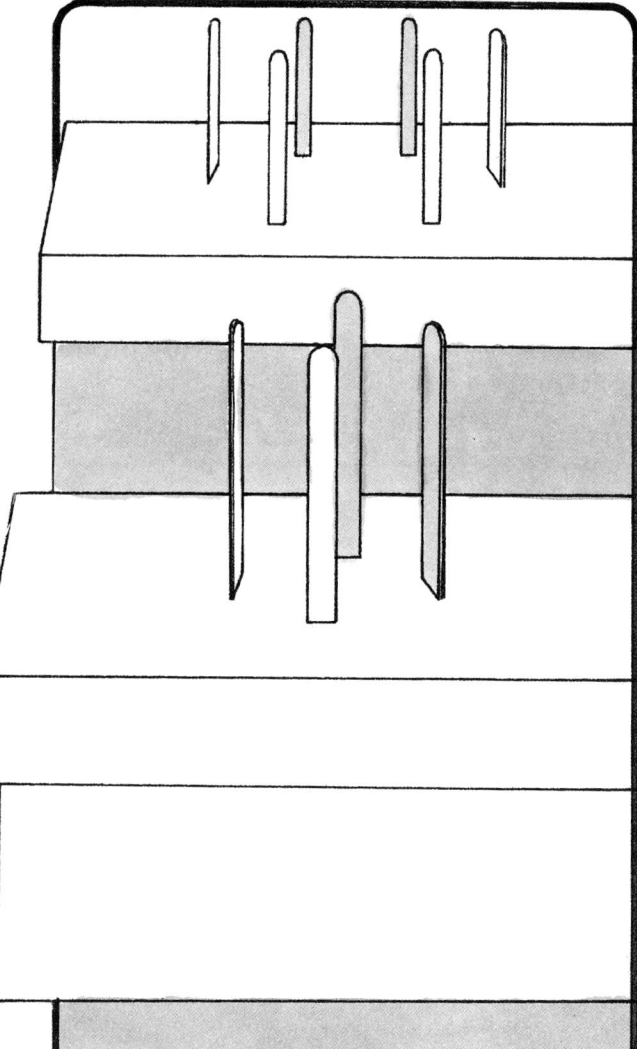

1 Set up the sticks or pencils on the box as shown, according to whether you have bar or horseshoe magnets. The sticks or pencils should be spaced slightly further apart than the size of the magnets they are going to contain. Push the sticks carefully into the box — top and bottom — so that they are held firmly.

2 Place one magnet between the sticks or pencils and place the other magnet on top. You must make sure that the north poles are at the same end (the south poles will then automatically be at the same end). If your magnets are not marked with north and south poles, don't worry. If you have got it wrong your magnets will click together showing that you positioned a north pole of one magnet with a south pole of the other. Simply turn one magnet round to get the like poles together.

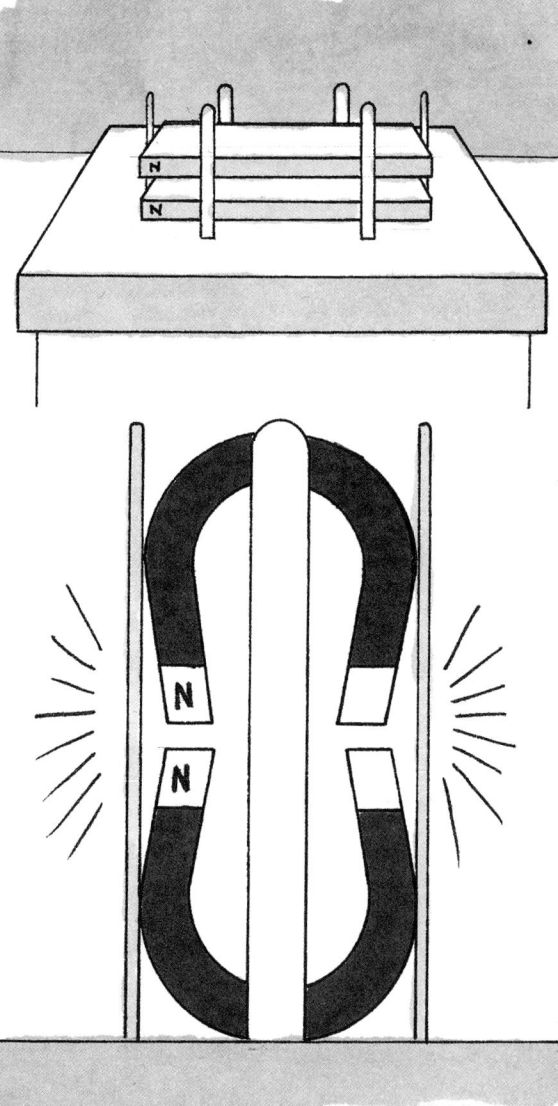

Look what happens. Instead of attracting each other, the magnets repel each other causing one magnet to be pushed away from the other and left floating in space.

What do magnets attract?

You probably know that magnets attract metal, but do they attract all metals? Can they attract through water or glass? Do some experiments to find out.

You Will Need
A magnet
Paper clips
A few coins
Silver foil
A glass of water

Place a few paper clips on the table. Bring your magnet near them. The clips will jump towards the magnet showing that they are attracted to it.

What happens if you try to attract coins, or silver foil? Try this experiment with various other metal objects and see what happens. Also, does the magnet attract through the table cloth or through a newspaper?

Now drop a few paper clips into the glass of water. Slowly lower the magnet into the water. Do the paper clips still jump towards the magnet? What happens if you place the magnet outside the glass and try and attract the paper clips?

Listen through wood

You Will Need
A wooden table
A pencil or watch
A friend

Sound travels better through wood than it does through air, for air is a poor conductor. To prove this, tap on a wooden table with the end of the pencil. Do this so gently that you can barely hear the sound. Now get your friend to tap and place your ear to the table about a metre or so from the tapping pencil. You will hear the sound more clearly, as you are not using air as the conductor of the sound, but are using wood instead. If you have a watch which has an audible tick (some modern watches make no sound) you can try this experiment using the watch placed on the table. What results do you get?

☆ Make a tin-can telephone

You Will Need
Heavy twine about 20 m long
2 empty tin cans (use tins that have had lids so there are no sharp edges)
A hammer and nail
A friend
An adult

1 Ask an adult to punch a hole in the bottom of each tin can using the hammer and nail.

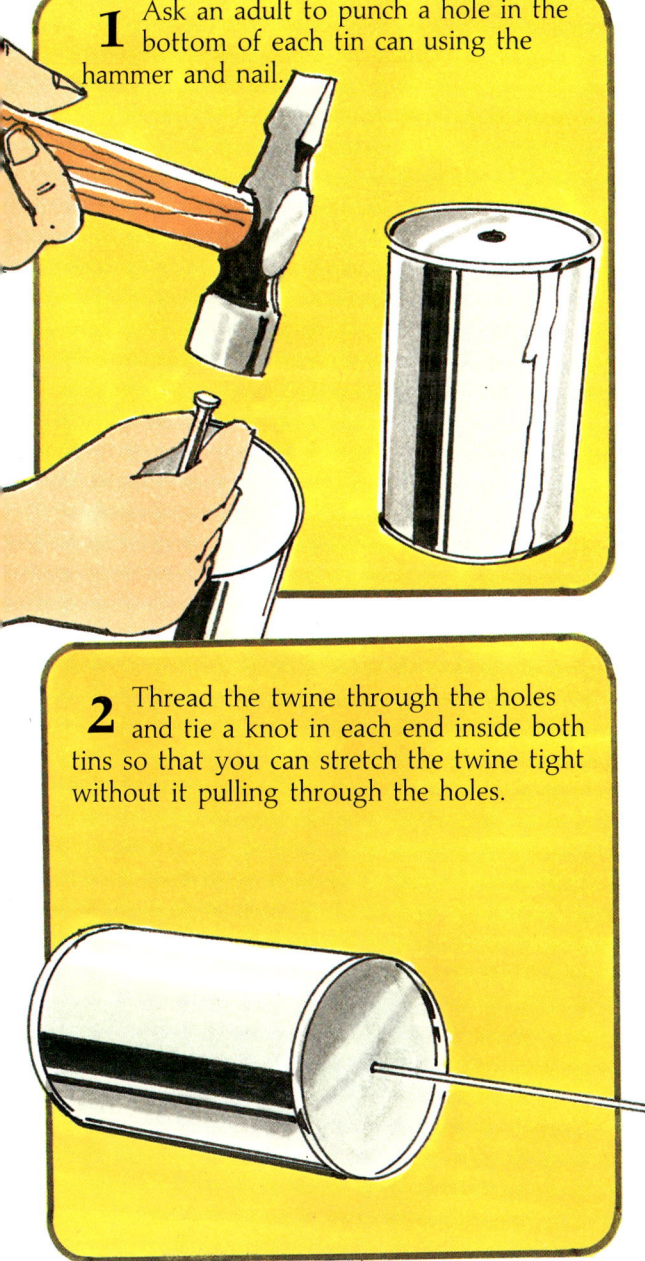

2 Thread the twine through the holes and tie a knot in each end inside both tins so that you can stretch the twine tight without it pulling through the holes.

3 Get a friend to walk as far away from you as he or she can with one tin so that the twine is stretched tight. Place the other tin to your ear. If your friend now speaks quietly into his or her tin, you will hear them very clearly. They will be able to hear you speaking quietly into your tin if you get them to place their tin to their ear.

4 Since you are talking very quietly — too quietly probably to hear your friend normally — this shows that a solid (in this case, string) conducts sound better than a gas (air).

☆ Make a photometer

A *photometer* is an instrument which measures the intensity or brightness of light. It compares an unknown source of light with a known one. Here is an easy way to make a simple one.

You Will Need
Plasticine
A small wooden board
Several candles
A piece of cardboard, white on *both* **sides (glue two pieces together if you have not got any cardboard which is white on both sides)**
2 pencils
A miniature lamp and socket and battery (or a torch without the reflector)
An adult

1 Make a groove in the block of wood that will hold the piece of white cardboard upright. The cardboard must be white on both sides. Put Plasticine in the groove to help hold it firmly. If you cannot make a groove, Plasticine alone will probably hold the card in place.

2 On each side of the cardboard, and 3.5 centimetres from it, make Plasticine mounds to hold the pencils, lead up. The pencils and their mounds must be on the same piece of wood which holds the cardboard. This apparatus you have now made is the photometer itself.

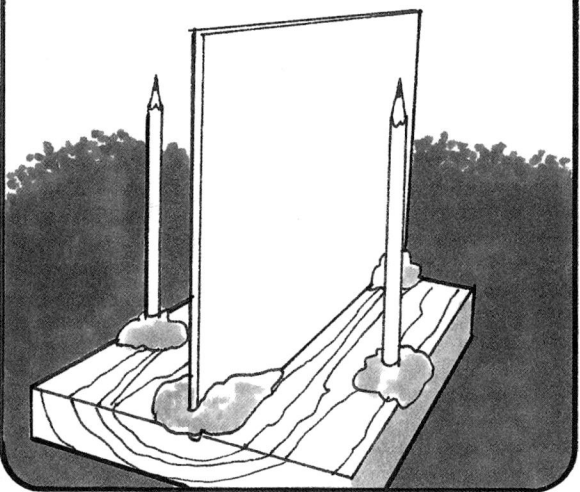

3 Make two mounds of plasticine to hold the candles, as shown in the illustration. Two of the candles should be very close together so they shine as one. The candles should all be about the same height to ensure that the light they produce is the same.

4 Place the double candle and the single candle about 60 centimetres apart with the photometer an equal distance between them.

5 Ask an adult to light the candles. One shadow on the cardboard screen will be darker than the other. Move the photometer back and forth until the shadows are equally dark. Notice that the photometer is about half as far from the single candle as it is from the two candles. This is because the single candle is only half the brightness of the two candles placed together.

When the photometer is an equal distance from the light sources and the shadows are equally dark, the sources are equally bright. Test a miniature lamp in a socket by substituting it for the single candle. Place it exactly as far from the photometer as the candles are placed on the other side. Add more candles until the shadows are equally dark. When this happens count the number of candles. You have found the candlepower of the lamp.

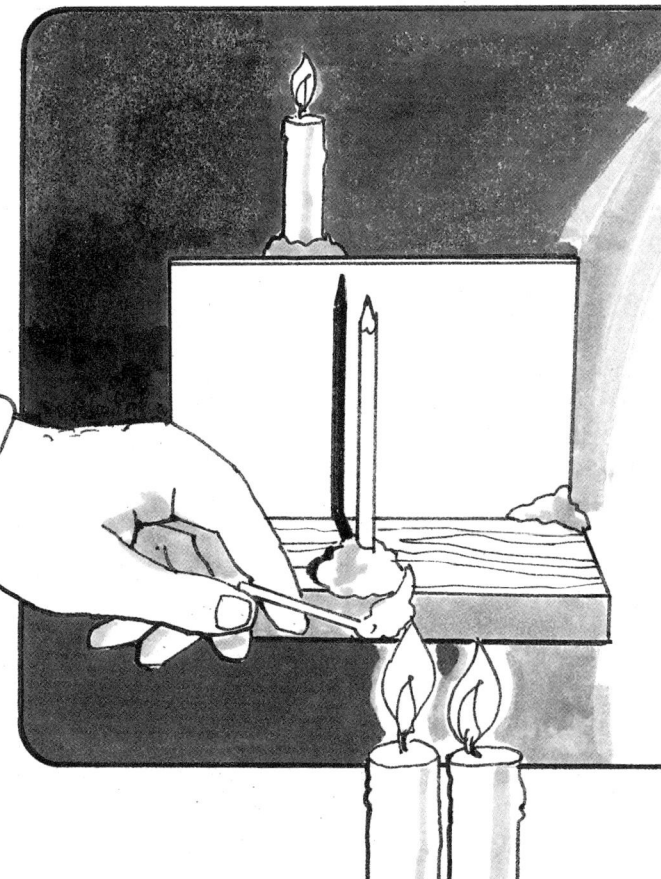

Magic with refracted light

When light travels from one medium to another, such as from air to water, it bends. The light still travels in a straight line, but in a different direction. Similarly, if the light travels from water to air, it will again change direction.

See how this works to perform magic.

You Will Need
A coin (a dark coloured coin is best)
An opaque bowl
Water
A friend

Place the coin in the centre of the empty opaque bowl. Look across the top of the bowl so you cannot see the penny; get into a position so that the coin is *just* out of your view. Now, stay in this position whilst a friend pours water into the bowl. Hey presto! You can suddenly see the coin.

Try this trick the other way round. With your coin still in the centre of the bowl and covered with water, raise yourself up so that you are over the top of the bowl, looking down on the coin. Now slowly lower yourself back towards the position you were in when you were looking across the top of the bowl.

As you move your head lower and lower, and still look at the coin, the coin will appear to move. It seems to be climbing up the side of the bowl. Suddenly it disappears completely. In fact, what has happened is that your head has reached a point where the surface of the water acts as a reflector and the light waves from the coin no longer reach your eyes thus preventing you from seeing it.

Make a kaleidoscope

Kaleidoscope is Greek for 'beautiful form'. The device uses mirrors and reflected light to produce the interesting shapes. It is easy to make one.

You Will Need

3 mirrors, the same size and shape,
  about 5 cm × 8 cm
Sticky tape
2 small panes of glass
Waxed paper
Coloured tissues
Several large books
A torch

1 Tape the three mirrors together along their longest sides, with the reflective surfaces facing inwards.

2 Cut a piece of waxed paper to fit over the top of the mirrors and tape it in position.

3 Set up the apparatus as shown in the illustration. One pane of glass should be placed on books so that it is about 25 centimetres from the ground or a table top. The second pane of glass should be 5 centimetres from the first pane. Arrange the books so that you have this distance between the panes.

4 Place some small pieces of coloured tissues (as many colours as you can) on the lower pane of glass. Shine a torch through the glass from underneath and look at the pieces of tissue through the top of the triangle of mirrors which is placed on the top pane of glass.

You will see many reflections of the tissues, and by moving the pieces of tissue around on the lower pane of glass you will see many interesting patterns through the top of the triangle of mirrors.

If you have some chips of coloured glass, you can use these instead of the pieces of tissue.

Make a pin-hole camera

A camera takes a photograph by allowing light to fall on to special chemically-treated light-sensitive paper for a certain amount of time. Getting the right amount of light and focusing the camera so that only certain images are in the photograph is what makes the world of photography so fascinating.

You Will Need

A cardboard box with a lid (a shoe box
  for example)
A pin or needle
Light-proof tape (dark masking tape
  should be satisfactory)
Sheets of black and white photographic
  film (available from a good
  photographic dealer)
A red bulb of low wattage (or a torch
  with red cellophane over the end)

1 Make a tiny hole in the centre of one end of the box using a pin or a needle. Put a small piece of tape over it on the outside of the box.

2 Put the red bulb into the light in a room. (Red light does not affect photographic film.) Make sure no other light comes into the room. Draw the curtains and seal up all cracks in the door. The best place to handle your film would be in a large cupboard, such as a broom cupboard, with a light.

3 In this room, tape a piece of photographic film inside the box opposite the hole. The side with chemically-treated paper (the shiny side) must face into the box. Tape the lid on to the box so that no light can get in.

4 Take your camera outside and place it about 2 metres in front of something you wish to photograph, eg a tree or a house. Rest the camera on something so that it doesn't move about. Quickly remove the tape from the pin-hole for a second and then replace it securely. Be careful not to stand in front of the pin-hole, or move the camera.

5 Take the camera back to the dark room, remove the photographic film and place it in a light-proof pack like the one it originally came in. When you have taken several photographs take them to your photographic dealer to be developed.

Try using different exposure times (the amount of time you removed the tape from the pin-hole for) and different light conditions, and see what results you get.

63

Make your own rainbow

Normal sunlight, or white light, is in fact made up of a variety of colours. You can often see these in a rainbow when the sunlight passes through water droplets in clouds during rainy weather.

You can create your own rainbow by allowing sunlight to shine through a glass of water. The water acts as a *prism* and breaks up the light just like the water droplets in clouds do.

You Will Need
A glass of water
A large sheet of white paper

Place the glass of water on a window sill where the sun is shining brightly. The glass must be slightly over the edge of the sill. Put the white paper on the floor below the window. You will see the light broken into its rainbow colours of violet, indigo, blue, green, yellow, orange and red.

Break up white light and put it together again

If you did the experiment on page 64 you will have seen how to turn white light into colours. In this experiment you will see how to use the colours to make white light.

You Will Need
A cardboard disc, about 10 cm diameter
Some coloured crayons (red, orange, yellow, green, blue, violet)
A flat-headed nail
Non-toxic glue
Hand drill

2 Push the nail through the centre and glue it in place.

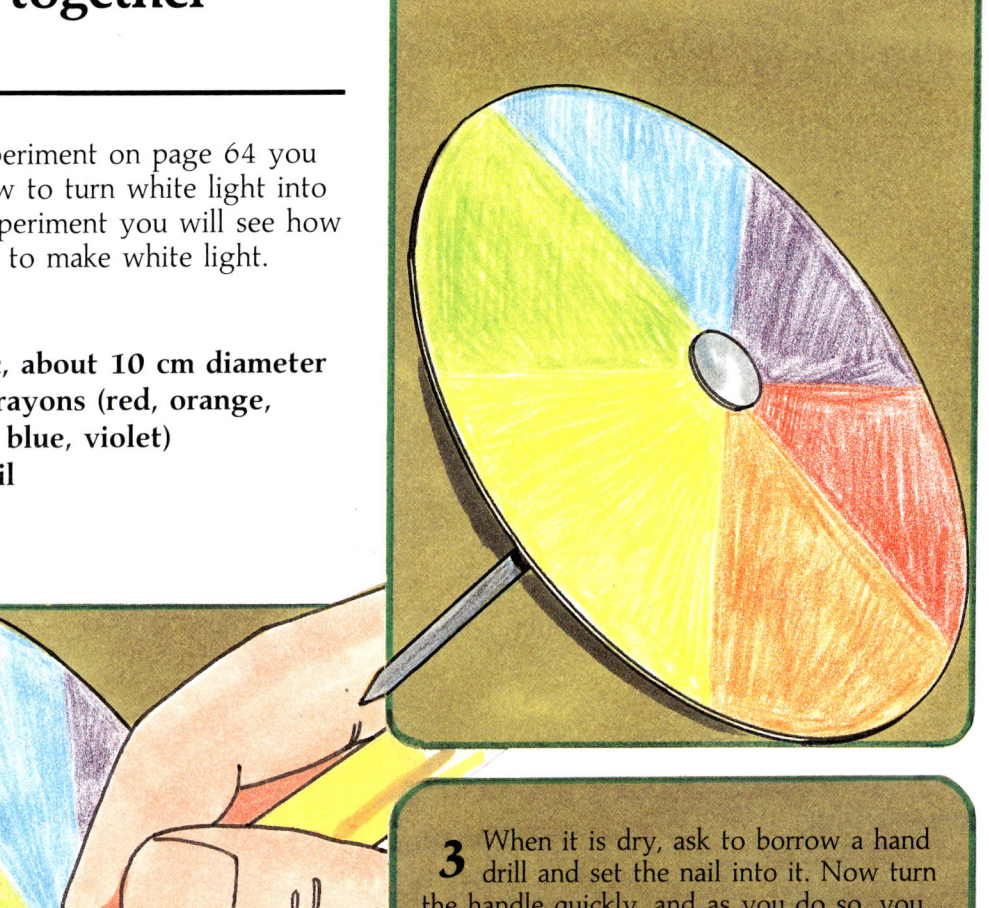

3 When it is dry, ask to borrow a hand drill and set the nail into it. Now turn the handle quickly, and as you do so, you will see the colours all blend together until the disc becomes pure white.

1 Cut out the disc and colour it in segments as shown.

☆ How does heat travel?

Heat will move from a warm object to a cool one. It will also move from the warm part of an object to a cooler part. Here's a simple experiment to prove it.

You Will Need
A candle
A metal tray
A steel knitting needle
A cork from a bottle
An adult

2 Ask an adult to light the candle and drip four or five blobs of equal sized wax on to the needle at 2.5-centimetre intervals, and place the lighted candle on the metal tray.

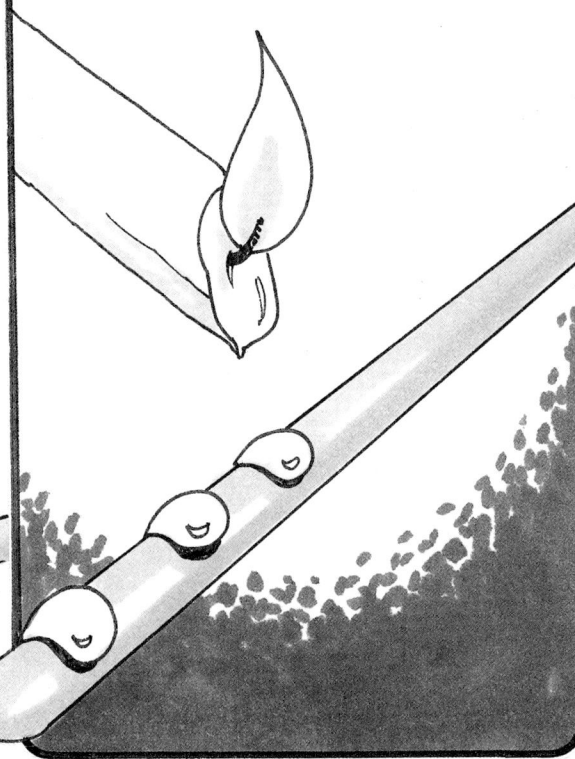

1 Push the pointed end of the knitting needle through the cork. Push the cork almost to the end of the knitting needle.

3 Hold the cork and put the end of the needle in the candle flame. Keep it steady and watch what happens.

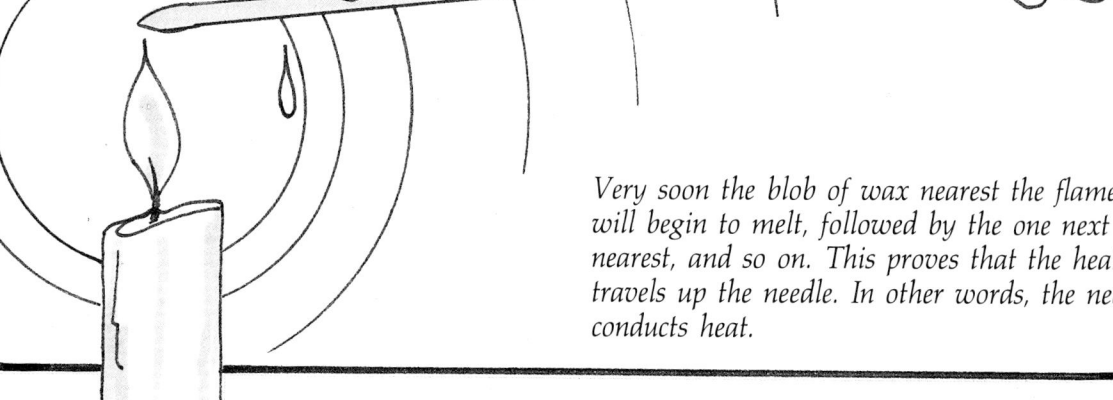

Very soon the blob of wax nearest the flame will begin to melt, followed by the one next nearest, and so on. This proves that the heat travels up the needle. In other words, the needle conducts heat.

☆ What is the best conductor of heat?

All materials conduct heat, but some are such poor conductors of heat that they are called insulators. An insulator is something that is better at stopping the transfer of heat than conducting it. Iron and steel are good conductors. Wood and air are poor conductors, but good insulators.

You can see this for yourself in the following experiment.

You Will Need
A long nail
A pencil
**2 strips of paper about 12 mm wide and
    20 cm long**
A candle
A metal tray
Tweezers or tongs
Non-toxic glue
An adult

1 Wrap one strip of paper diagonally around the nail and one around the pencil. Secure the free ends with a dab of glue and let the glue dry.

2 Ask an adult to light the candle and secure it on a metal tray.

3 Get your adult to hold the tip of the paper-wrapped nail in the tweezers, placing the other end in the candle flame. Note how long it takes for the paper to char and then burn. Repeat the experiment, this time using the pencil.

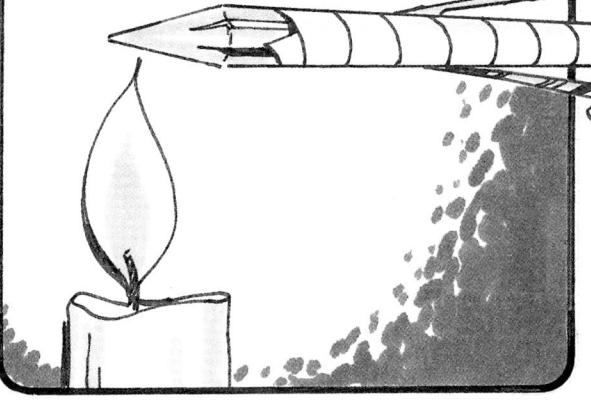

The paper wrapped round the nail took longer to burn because the nail, being a good heat conductor, took the heat from the paper for a while. The pencil — a poor conductor — was not able to conduct much heat away and so the paper around it began to char almost immediately after it was put into the candle flame.

Bring the Sun down to size

How big is the Sun compared with the Earth? And how far away is it? Here's a simple way to see for yourself.

You Will Need

A green crayon or pen
A blue crayon or pen
A yellow crayon or pen
A piece of plain paper or card about 15 cm long
A piece of plain paper or card at least 35 cm square
A ruler or tape measure

Draw a green circle about 4 millimetres across on the paper. This represents the Earth. Now make a blue dot on the same piece of paper, about 9.5 centimetres from the green circle. This represents the Moon. In reality the Moon is 384 000 kilometres (239 000 miles) away from the Earth, but this is how they appear in size and distance on this small scale.

Now, on another piece of paper, draw a yellow circle 33 centimetres across. This represents the Sun. Go outside, or to a park, and place the paper with the yellow circle somewhere where you can see it from some distance, or get a friend to hold it. Place the other piece of paper 26 metres away from the 'Sun'. Now you will have some idea how far the Sun is from the Earth, and how big it is in relation to the Earth and Moon. In fact, the Sun is over 149 000 000 kilometres (93 000 000 miles) from the Earth.

Jupiter

Relative sizes of the planets

Saturn

Uranus

Neptune

Venus

Mercury

Earth

Sun

Jupiter

Mars

Saturn

Uranus

Neptune

Pluto

Solar System

Is it going to rain?

Some plants and animals show you when it is going to rain. They are not all reliable, but then nor are the official weather forecasts! Watch out for these signs and see if they were right.

Pine cones close before rain.

Earthworms leave their burrows in moist air conditions and may be seen at the surface.

Horses and cattle can often tell when its going to rain, and they gather on the leeward side (the side away from the wind) of hedges and trees. Cattle often lie down in fields before rain.

Black garden beetles — sometimes called rain beetles — can often be seen on the surface of the soil prior to a storm.

Rooks gather near their rookeries when rain clouds appear.

Make a rain gauge

You Will Need

A jam jar
A funnel, the same width as the jam jar at its widest point (if you haven't got one the right size, you can still make a rain gauge without it)
A tall, narrow jar
A ruler
Paint
A small paint brush
Water

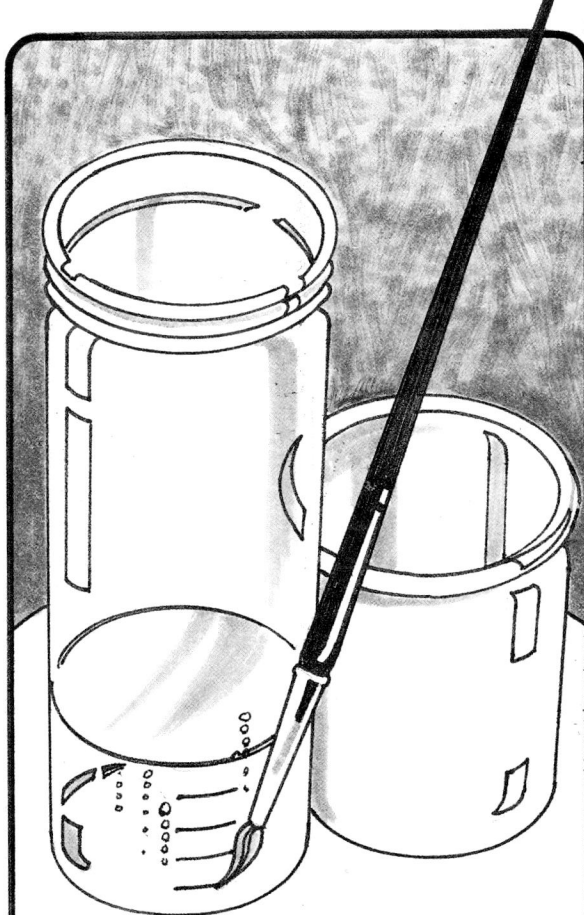

1 First, pour exactly 2.5 centimetres of water into the jam jar. Now carefully pour it into the narrow jar and divide the length of the column of water into 5 equal parts. Each part will now represent 5 millimetres. Mark the 5-millimetre points on the jar with the paint and allow to dry. This will then be your measuring jar.

2 Take the empty jam jar and push it into the soil so that the neck is level with the soil. Place the funnel in the jar. If you have a plastic funnel, it may be possible to trim a little off the top until it is the same width as the jar. If you cannot get the two widths the same, do not use the funnel; your gauge will still work quite well.

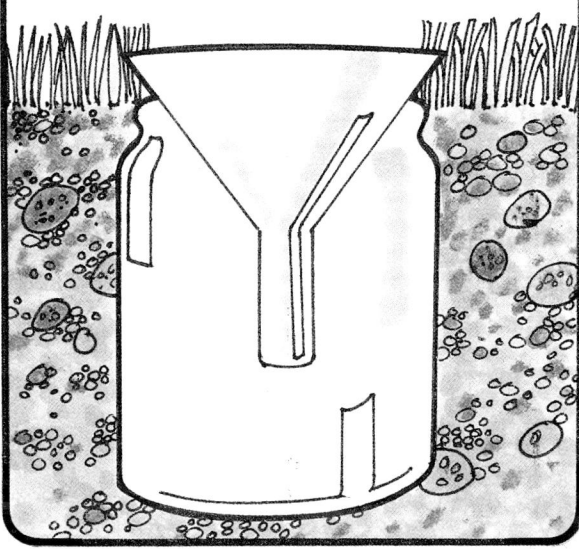

3 When it rains, drops will collect in your jam jar. Afterwards, pour the rain water into the measuring jar and measure how much rain has fallen.

You can take a record every day and see how the rainfall varies throughout the year. (If you find more than 2.5 centimetres of rain is falling, mark your measuring jar with extra divisions.)

Make a barometer

A *barometer* is an instrument which measures the pressure of the air. This pressure is called *atmospheric pressure*. Here is how to make one.

You Will Need
A tall glass jar
A balloon
Scissors
A rubber band
A drinking straw
White card
Non-toxic glue (*not* **plastic cement type**)
A pencil

1 Cut a piece out of the balloon and stretch it over the mouth of the jar.

2 Twist the rubber band around the neck of the jar and the stretched balloon several times to keep the balloon tightly in place.

3 Place a drop of glue in the centre of the stretched balloon (be sure not to use glue which dissolves rubber, or your work will be wasted). Hold one end of the straw on the glue until it dries so that it is stuck to the balloon as shown.

4 Write HIGH and LOW on the white card and stick it somewhere so that it can be behind the free end of the straw.

You now have a barometer. As the pressure of the air increases, it presses hard in all directions. It presses hard on the jar all over as well as on the balloon surface, pushing it downward. The end of the straw on the balloon dips down too, causing the other end to point upward to HIGH.

When the air pressure is low it does not press so hard on objects. If the pressure within the jar has more force pushing upwards than the outside pressure pushing downwards the result is that the balloon bulges upwards, causing the free end of the straw to dip down, pointing to LOW.

A rapid drop in pressure usually means that bad weather is on the way.

☆ Make a wind vane

If you want to know which way the wind is blowing, you should have a wind vane.

You Will Need
Some stiff cardboard
Non-toxic glue
Scissors
A large pin or nail
An old broom handle
A drill
A compass
An adult

1 Draw, and then cut out, an arrow shape from the cardboard, as illustrated, and carefully push the pin, smeared with a little glue, through the central point of the arrow. (You can find the centre by balancing the arrow on your finger. Your finger will be in the middle when the arrow balances.)

2 Ask an adult to drill a hole slightly larger than the pin or nail in one end of the broom handle. The hole must be deep enough for the pin to fit snugly, but must be shallower than the distance from the bottom of the arrow to the bottom of the pin, as shown in the illustration.

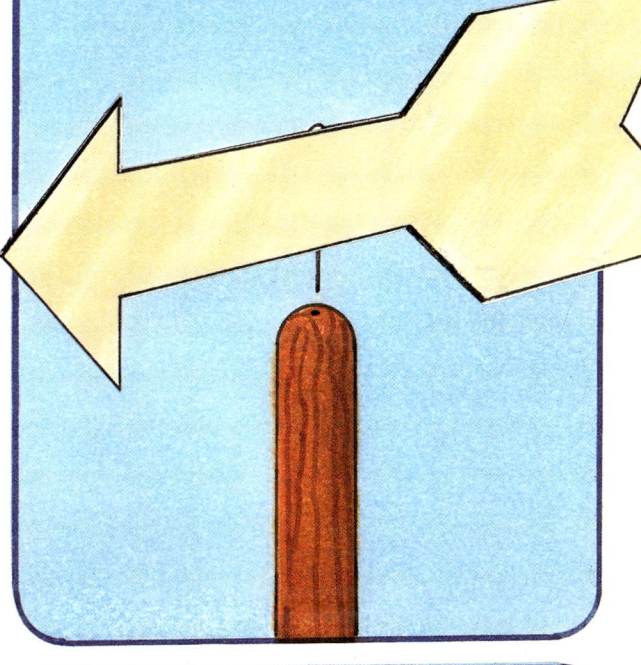

3 Push the other end of the broom handle into the ground and insert the arrow in the hole in the top. The arrow will swing round until it is pointing into the wind. Use the compass to find out in what direction it is pointing. If the arrow points to the west, there is a westerly wind blowing.

☆ Make an anemometer

A gauge which measures how fast the wind is blowing is called an *anemometer*. Here's how to make one. **Ask an adult to help you with all the stages.**

You Will Need
2 rubber balls
A sharp knife or scissors
2 pieces of wood about 45 cm long and 2 cm thick
A piece of wood about 60 cm long and 2.5 cm thick
A block of wood 15 cm square
A nail about 6 cm long
Short nails
A hammer
A drill
Paint, a different colour to the balls
Sticky tape
Vaseline or grease
An adult

1 Cut the balls in half. Paint one of the halves so you can see it easily when the anemometer turns.

2 Nail a half-ball to each end of both the 45-centimetre-long pieces of wood, as shown.

3 Hammer the long nail through the middle of the two pieces at right angles, and tape them to prevent them working loose. Nail the 60-centimetre-long piece of wood on to the block by nailing through the block, using some of the short nails. Drill a hole a little larger than the thickness of the long nail, in the top of the long piece of wood. It should be just deep enough so that the nail sits snugly in the hole but with a slight gap between the long piece of wood and the other pieces.

4 Grease the long nail so that it spins freely in the hole.

5 Place your anemometer on the ground outside where it can be blown by the wind. To measure the speed of the wind count the number of times a ball goes round in half a minute — you will find it easier if you keep an eye on the painted ball — and divide by 3. This will give you the approximate speed of the wind in kilometres per hour. (Divide by 5 for miles per hour.)

Use the Beaufort wind scale

There is a way to tell the approximate speed of the wind without using an *anemometer*, and that is to use the Beaufort scale devised by Sir Francis Beaufort. It refers to the effect on everyday objects.

No	TITLE	EFFECT OF WIND	KM/H
0	Calm	SMOKE RISES VERTICALLY	less than 1
1.	Light Air	SMOKE DRIFTS, VANE DOESN'T TURN	1-5
2.	Light Breeze	LEAVES RUSTLE VANE MOVES	6-11
3.	Gentle Breeze	LIGHT FLAG EXTENDS	12-19
4.	Moderate Breeze	DUST AND LOOSE PAPER RAISED	20-29

No	TITLE	EFFECT OF WIND	KM/H
5.	Fresh Breeze	SMALL TREES SWAY	30-39
6.	Strong Breeze	LARGE BRANCHES IN MOTION	40-50
7.	Moderate Gale	WHOLE TREES IN MOTION	51-61
8.	Fresh Gale	TWIGS BROKEN OFF TREES	62-74
9.	Strong Gale	CHIMNEY POTS AND SLATES REMOVED	75-87
10.	Whole Gale	TREES UPROOTED	88-101
11.	Storm	WIDESPREAD DAMAGE	102-120
12.	Hurricane	DEVASTATION	Above 121

Make a high-altitude wind gauge

The direction of the wind high above the Earth may be different from its direction at the Earth's surface. Weather-observers should keep records of the wind's direction high in the sky as well as near the ground. One way of finding the direction of winds high above the Earth is to note the direction in which the clouds are moving. The wind is blowing them towards that direction so it is blowing from the opposite direction. This is how you can build your own cloud-watching device. It is called a *nephoscope*.

You Will Need

A circular or square mirror, about 15 cm across
A piece of cardboard 20 cm square
Red paint or nail varnish
Drawing compasses, including pencil
A magnetic compass (see pages 52–3)
Non-toxic glue

1 Draw a circle, with a diameter exactly equal to the diameter of the mirror, in the centre of the cardboard. If you use a square mirror, the diameter of the circle should be equal to a diagonal of the mirror.

2 Place a dab of glue in the centre of the circle and stick the back of the mirror to the circle. Wait several hours for the glue to dry.

3 Place a small dab of nail polish or paint in the exact centre of the front of the mirror.

4 Make a mark on the cardboard near the mirror and label it N for north. Directly opposite north, mark S for south. Half-way between, on opposite sides, mark W for west and E for east. Half-way between these marks, mark off NE, SE, NW, SW in the proper places.

5 To use your nephoscope, place it outdoors on a level surface. Using the magnetic compass, place the mirror so that the N mark on the cardboard faces exactly north. Watch in the mirror for the reflection of a passing cloud. When the cloud passes over the mark in the centre of the mirror, track the cloud's path. Note in which direction it passed off the mirror. That is the direction *towards* which the wind is blowing high in the sky. It is blowing *from* the opposite direction.

If you have also made the wind indicator on page 73, you can see whether the wind direction at ground level is the same as that at high altitude on any particular day.

☆ Make a hygrometer

A *hygrometer* is an instrument used to measure humidity – the amount of moisture in the air.

On a humid day, hair stretches and lengthens. On a dry day, hair contracts. Since changes in the amount of moisture in the air affect the length of human hair, you can use hair to measure moisture or humidity. Here is how to make a hair hygrometer.

You Will Need

A piece of wood about 30 cm long
A block of wood about 15 cm square
An empty cotton reel
A wooden rod (It should fit through the cotton reel so that the reel turns fairly easily on it.)
A large drinking straw
Nails
A piece of cardboard about 15 cm square
Drawing pins
Scissors
A pencil
Sticky tape
A long, straight, freshly-washed, blond hair (use a blond hair if possible as it will stretch more)
An adult

1 Ask an adult to make a wooden stand similar to the one in the picture.

2 Fasten the hair with a drawing pin or sticky tape to the side of the stand and run it over the reel.

3 Attach the cardboard to the base of the stand to draw a scale on.

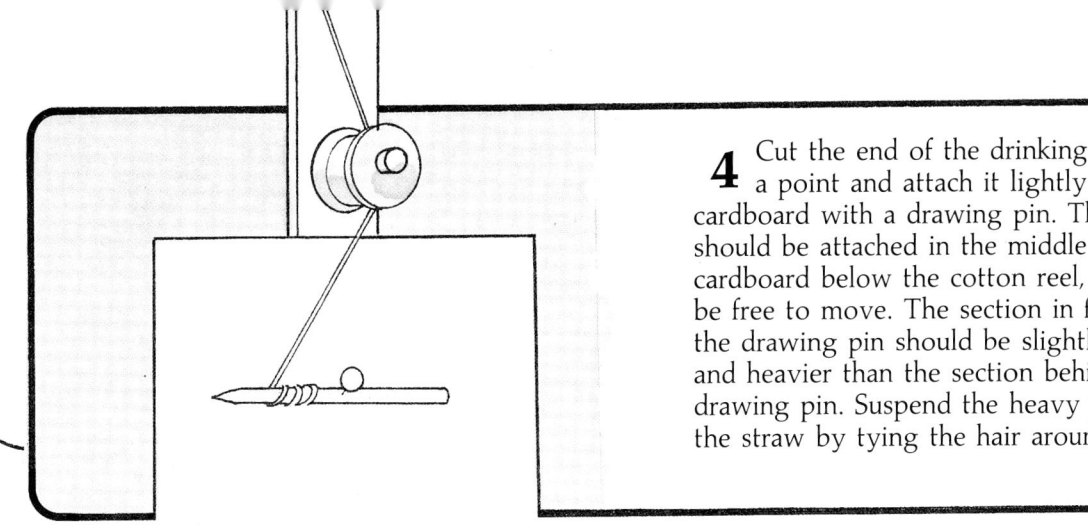

4 Cut the end of the drinking straw to a point and attach it lightly to the cardboard with a drawing pin. The straw should be attached in the middle of the cardboard below the cotton reel, and must be free to move. The section in front of the drawing pin should be slightly longer and heavier than the section behind the drawing pin. Suspend the heavy part of the straw by tying the hair around it.

5 Wet a towel with hot water and suspend it carefully over the instrument. Leave it for a few minutes. Remove it and quickly mark on the cardboard where the straw is pointing. This will indicate high humidity. The hair should have stretched and permitted the pointer to fall. Now make the hair very, very dry by leaving the instrument near a radiator, hot air vent or fire for several hours. Mark the spot where the straw is pointing. It should be pointing upwards. Mark this line for low humidity. Mark off sections between these two marks to make your scale.

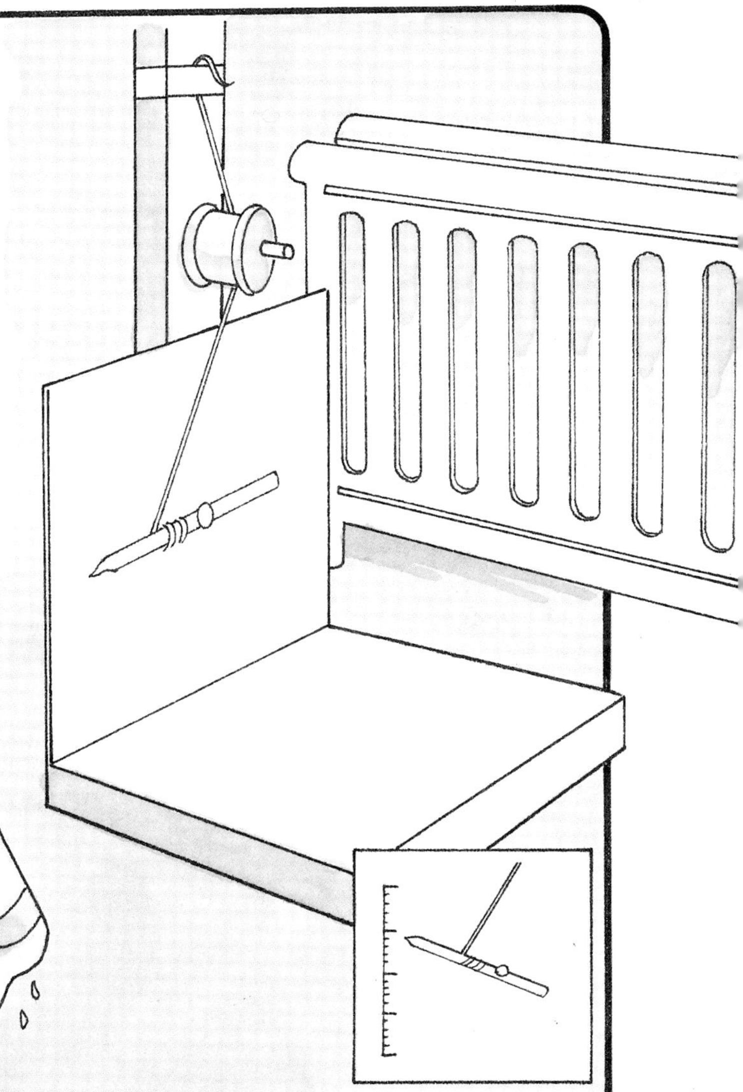

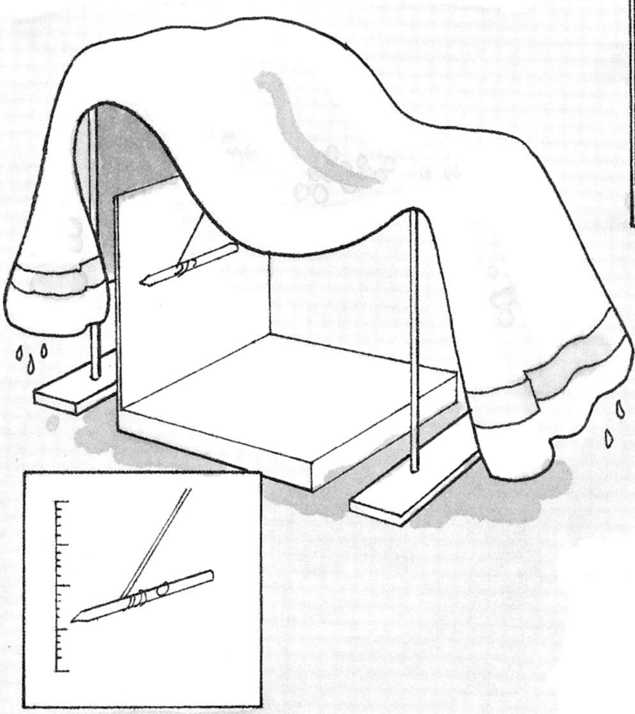

This instrument will not give you an exact relative humidity reading, but it will indicate changes in the humidity. Keep a record of humidity on different days.

Have your own weather station

You Will Need
An anemometer (see page 74)
A wind vane (see page 73)
A rain gauge (see page 71)
A barometer (see page 72)
A high-altitude wind gauge (see pages 76–7)
A hygrometer (see pages 78–9)
A thermometer (to measure air temperature)
A large sheet of paper
A pencil
A ruler

If you have made all of these pieces of weather-indicating equipment, all you need to obtain is a thermometer to measure air temperature, and you have all you need to make your own weather station. Place your thermometer outside to take readings. When it snows, measure the depth of snow by placing a ruler into *fresh* snow until it reaches the ground, and then record the level. If you want to calculate the amount of water, remember that 25 centimetres of snow equals 2.5 centimetres of rain water.

Do not measure a snow drift, for this gives a falsely high reading. Draw a chart on the paper, like the one shown here, and add the different measurements to it as you take your readings.

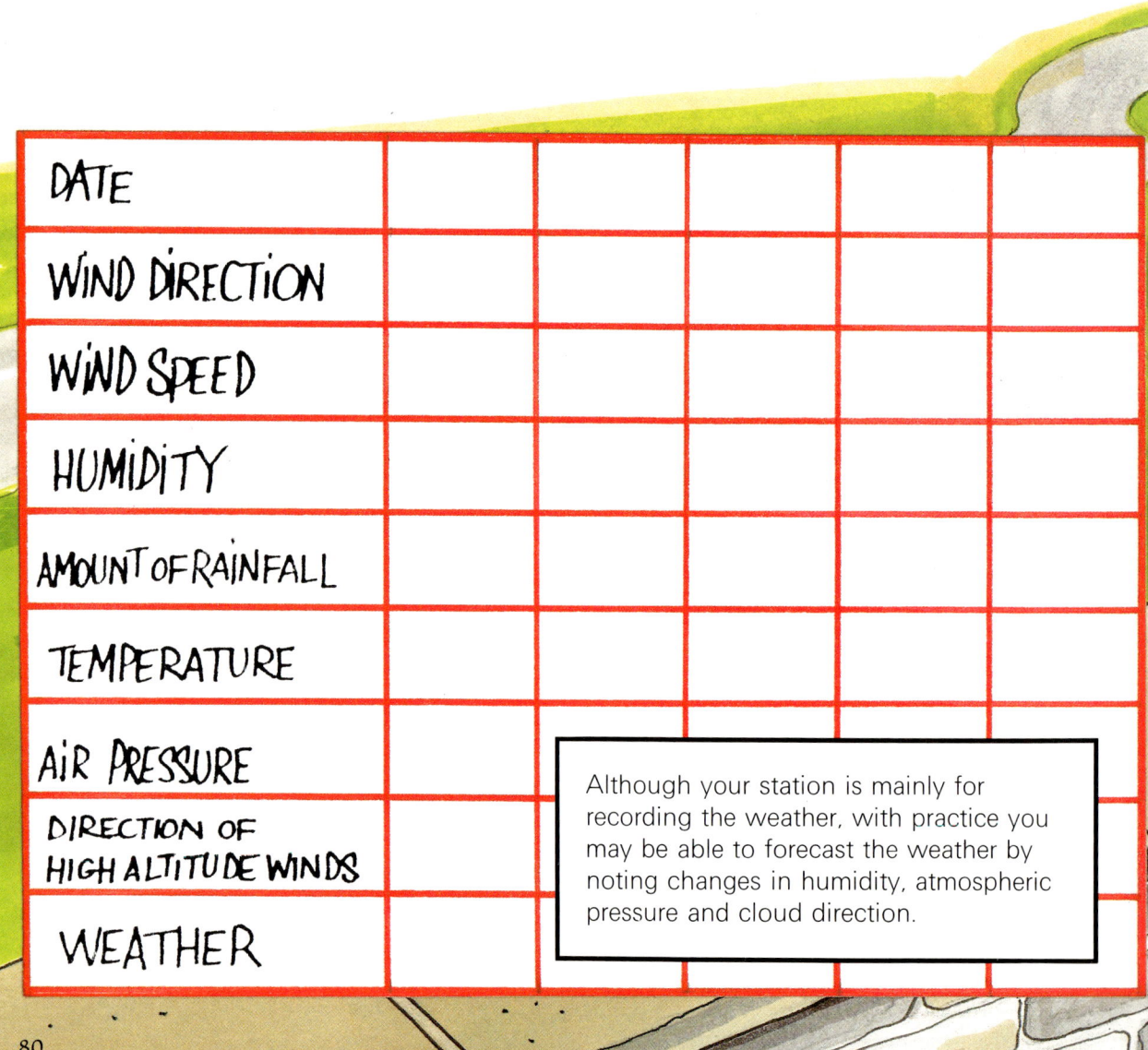

DATE					
WIND DIRECTION					
WIND SPEED					
HUMIDITY					
AMOUNT OF RAINFALL					
TEMPERATURE					
AIR PRESSURE					
DIRECTION OF HIGH ALTITUDE WINDS					
WEATHER					

Although your station is mainly for recording the weather, with practice you may be able to forecast the weather by noting changes in humidity, atmospheric pressure and cloud direction.

What is snow made of?

After a good fall of snow you might wonder how it will ever disappear — it seems so thick. In fact, snow is really water, and there is less of it than you think.

You Will Need
A straight-sided jar or drinking glass
Snow
A ruler

Next time it snows, collect some snow in a tall glass jar. Fill it to the top, but do not pack it in tight. Now put the jar somewhere warm until the snow melts. How much snow — or rather water — have you got? Not very much. The snow was really ice crystals with air in between them.

Look at soil

There are many different kinds of soil, and any particular type of soil will contain all sorts of different sized particles. Different soils also have different characteristics. Sandy soils are *light* and free draining. This means that water runs through them quickly. Sometimes they are *too* free draining, and valuable minerals are washed away before the plants can make use of them. Clay soils are *heavy*. The particles are close together, unlike sandy soils, and water is held for a long time, often waterlogging the plants' roots and depriving them of air. The ideal soil is one between these two, and is known as a *loam*. Do these experiments to see what different soils are like.

You Will Need
A milk bottle
A plastic funnel
Cotton wool
A jam jar
Sand
Clay
Water
Soil

Seeing how soil is composed

1 Put about 4 centimetres of soil in a milk bottle.

2 Fill the bottle three-quarters full of water. Shake vigorously with your hand over the end.

3 Leave it to settle, and then look to see what has happened. The soil will have separated into distinct layers. Note that the heaviest particles are on the bottom and the lightest ones are nearest the top. You will be able to see the amounts of stony, sandy and clay particles.

How water drains through sand and clay

1 Place the funnel in the empty jam jar. Plug the funnel with cotton wool.

2 Put a measured amount of sand into the funnel. Pour on a measured amount of water, and note how long it takes the water to drain through into the jam jar.

3 Repeat the experiment using the same sized piece of cotton wool, the same amount of clay and the same amount of water. How does the drainage time compare with the time it took for the water to drain through the sand?

Do the experiment on soil composition using an equal amount of a different soil, and compare the contents.

What is it going to be?

You Will Need
A screw-cap jar and lid
Soil
Pupae

If you dig the soil over during autumn and winter, you may come across some cigar-shaped brown or red objects a few centimetres long. These are insect *pupae*, and they form after insects such as moths and butterflies have laid eggs which then turn into caterpillars. The pupa is the resting stage between the caterpillar and the adult.

If you find any pupae, put them in the jar and cover them with soil. Replace the lid, after making air holes in it, and store it in a cool place. In time, the pupae will turn into adults, which you will probably discover flitting angrily about in the jar. Try to identify them, before releasing them.

Nature's gardeners

Earthworms spend their lives burrowing through the soil and, as they do so, they help to mix together the humus from the surface with the soil beneath, and provide valuable air for the roots of the plants.

You can set up a wormery yourself to see just how effective worms are at mixing soil together.

You Will Need
A jam jar
Soil
Sand
A wine glass
Brown paper
An elastic band
A few small leaves
Some earthworms

1 Fill the jam jar with alternate layers of soil and sand, making each layer as even as you can.

2 Flatten the soil with something such as the bottom of a wine glass.

3 Cover the outside of the jar with brown paper, and put one or two small leaves on the top of the soil.

4 Put four or five earthworms on the top of the leaves. Keep the jar in a cool place and make sure that the soil does not become too dry by moistening the top with a few drops of water each day.

5 After a week, remove the brown paper. The earthworms will have mixed up all the soil by their burrowing, and will have pulled the leaves beneath the surface. Remember to release the worms after the experiment.

What do insects like best?

Many insects, such as bees, visit flowers to drink the sugary nectar which is produced at the base of the petals. Other insects — flies for instance — are less attracted by the sweet nectar, but prefer to feed on food such as rotting meat. You can set up your own experiment to see what sort of food attracts different insects.

You Will Need
5 saucers or dishes the same colour
Coloured card
Milk
Water
Sugar
Salt
Jam
A small piece of rotting meat
Paper
A pencil

Choose a sunny day when there will be lots of insects about, and place the five saucers on the ground near each other. A piece of coloured card underneath each dish will help the insects spot the dishes, but the card you use must be the same size and colour for each dish. In one dish put some milk, in the next some sugar solution, the next some salt solution, the next some jam, and the last one some rotting meat. Remember which dish contains salt and which sugar.

Write on a piece of paper 'salt', 'sugar', 'jam', 'milk' and 'meat'. All you have to do now is to wait and see which sorts of insects visit each dish, and how many times. Keep a record and, after an hour or so, consider your results.

Make your own pond

Making your own pond is not difficult, and it's great fun to watch all the creatures going about their daily lives, just as they would in a real pond. The pond we are going to make isn't the type that you build in the garden, because that involves lots of digging and waterproofing. You may already have an old fish tank at home, or you can buy one quite cheaply from a pet shop. Whatever you choose to make your pond with, you should remember to try to copy the conditions of a natural pond.

You Will Need

A fish tank or large basin
Glue to seal cracks with (silicone rubber cement)
Sand
Stones
Jam jars
A long-handled net
Pond water (Tap water is all right if you cannot find any pond water.)
Pond plants
Mud from the bottom of a pond
Pond animals

1 Make sure the tank is clean and does not leak. Seal any cracks you find. Place the tank on a strong table or shelf, out of direct sunlight.

2 Cover the bottom of the tank with clean, washed sand to a depth of about 2 centimetres. Put some clean, washed stones in to provide places for tiny creatures to hide.

3 Fill the tank with water and add some pond plants such as pondweed, hornwort or milfoil. These can be rooted into the sand or secured with stones to stop them floating about. The plants will help to provide oxygen for the animals.

4 Sprinkle half a jam jar full of mud into the water. This will help the animals to feel at home, and may also contain the eggs or larvae of pond animals that you can watch as they grow. Leave the tank to 'settle' for at least 48 hours.

5 With the long-handled net and jam jars, search carefully in a pond for some small creatures to put in your pond. Be careful not to fall in. Don't collect too many animals. Carnivorous animals like diving beetles, dragonfly nymphs and sticklebacks will soon eat most of the other inhabitants of your pond, so you must either keep them separately or choose less predatory animals. A good selection for your tank would be snails, newts, caddis larvae, tubifex worms, water fleas and shrimps. These can be collected from a pond by dipping your net near the bottom, under water lilies and among water weeds.

6 Bring your animals home in jam jars full of water as soon as you can and put them in the tank. Don't forget that your pond inhabitants will be much more healthy if they are not overcrowded. Feed them on a few fragments of chopped raw meat and vegetables. Don't leave any uneaten food or dead animals to rot in the tank, as this will kill the other animals. Remember to top up the water level whenever it becomes low.

tadpole

minnow

water scorpion

damsel fly larva

ramshorn snail

caddis fly larva

water beetle

There is no reason why your pond inhabitants should not continue to live happily for a long time, and provide you with many hours of enjoyable study. If you can fit your tank with an air pump to provide extra oxygen, it will be particularly appreciated by fish.

Here are a few of the things you may see: snails creeping about among the weeds or on the sides of the tank, rasping off pieces of food with their tongues; caddis larvae creeping about on the bottom, protected inside their tubes made of stones and twigs; water beetles swimming by using their flattened legs like oars; nest-building behaviour of sticklebacks; dragonfly nymphs stalking their prey and shooting out their face 'mask' to catch the victims; frog spawn, if you collected some from the pond in spring, turning into tadpoles and then into tiny frogs. (You will need to take the frogs out of your pond as soon as they have grown their legs and lost their tails, and release them back by the pond.)

smooth newt

great diving beetle

great pond snail

stickleback

Make a bird bath

Birds like to bathe; it gets dust and parasites out of their feathers and thus helps them stay fit and healthy. Sometimes you may see birds lining up for a bath in a small puddle, pecking each other as they wait impatiently in the queue.

You can easily make a bird bath in your own garden or on any piece of waste ground close by to where you live.

You Will Need
A spade
Tough plastic sheeting
Some large stones
Gravel

Choose a place which is away from bushes, or cats will be able to creep up on the birds unseen. Dig a small hole about a metre across and about 20 centimetres deep. Line the hole with the plastic sheeting and weight the edge down with large stones and then cover the edge and stones with some soil.

If you have a little gravel, place this in the bottom of the bath and then fill it up with water. You will need to ensure that the bath does not become filled with leaves in the autumn, and that it does not become too dry in summer.

Soon the birds will come to know of your bird bath, and you can have many hours of enjoyment watching their antics. Try to identify the different birds which come to bathe.

What did the owl eat?

Owls catch and eat a variety of animals, but they cannot digest some of the parts such as bones and feathers. Instead, they cast these up in a sort of lump called a *pellet*. Owl pellets can often be found under trees or near old buildings known to be used by owls. If you examine a pellet you will find out what the owl ate.

You Will Need

A dish of warm water
Tweezers
Non-toxic glue
A piece of black cardboard
A sewing needle

Soak the pellet in the warm water until it becomes loose. Leave it in the dish and gently separate the pellet using the tweezers and needle. You will probably find bones and some bits of feather. Only the bones are worth keeping. Clean these up and glue them on to the piece of cardboard. You may be able to identify the animals that the owl had eaten. Look in particular for the skulls of tiny mammals like mice and voles, and the beaks of small birds.

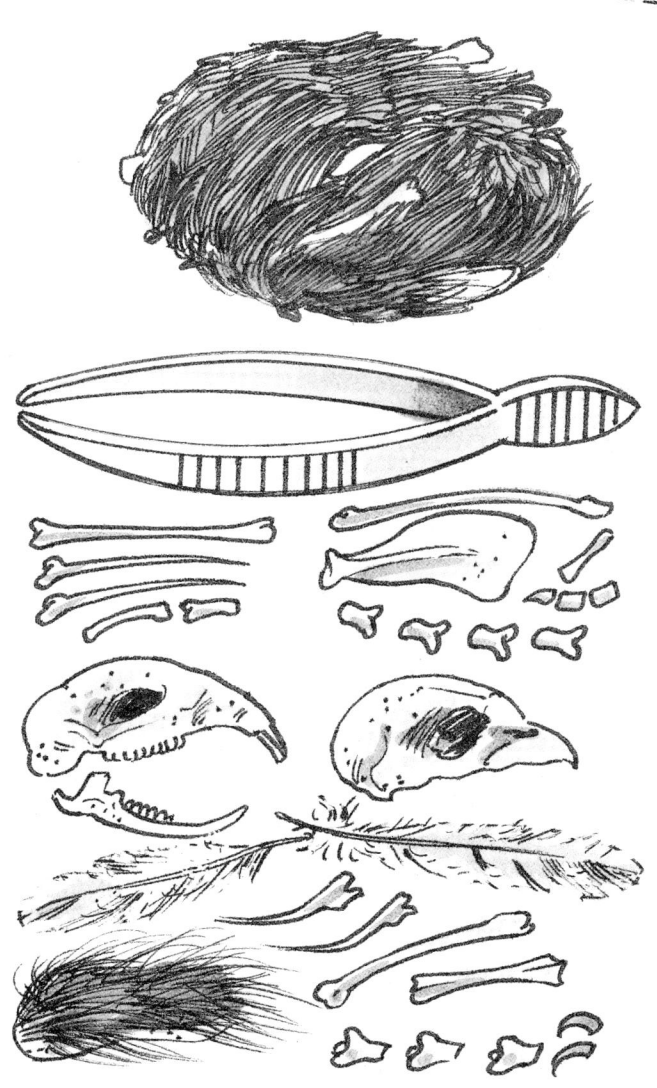

☆ What do birds like best?

In spring and summer there is plenty of natural food for birds to eat, but in the winter they are very grateful for any food put out for them. It is often the only thing that stops birds starving. A bird table in your garden will not only help keep birds alive, but will fill your garden with colour and interest during the winter months. You will be able to learn much about bird behaviour, too. If you cannot have a bird table, you can still scatter bacon scraps, fat, seed or bread crumbs on the ground and watch the birds feeding.

thrush

pied wagtail

nuthatch

robin

blue tit

sparrow

bullfinch

Wooden post 1½ m long

**1 piece of wood 40 cm × 40 cm × 1
 cm thick**

**4 pieces of wood 39 cm long, and about
 5 mm square**

A hammer

Nails

An adult

A notebook

Food for the birds

Ask an adult to build a bird table, by nailing
the pieces of wood together as shown in the
illustration. You will need to have a point at
one end of the post. The timber merchant
can cut one for you. The strips of wood
around the edge help prevent the food
blowing away, and the gaps allow water to
drain away when it rains.

Place the table with food on it where birds
can see the food easily, but away from
places where cats can creep up on the birds
unseen. Keep a notebook, and try to
observe the following: how long each bird
stays at the table; how many different birds
visit your table; if one bird is usually more
dominant than others; if for instance, seeds
are more favoured than bacon rind or
breadcrumbs.

Make plaster casts of twigs and footprints

You can make a permanent record of any tracks or footprints you find, by taking a plaster cast, and you can cast objects like twigs.

You Will Need
Clay or Plasticine
Plaster of Paris
Water
Cardboard
Sticky tape
Grease or vaseline
A spoon
A bowl to mix the plaster of Paris
A twig and/or footprint

Make a plaster cast of a twig

1 Mould the clay or Plasticine into a flattish block, large enough to take the shape of your twig.

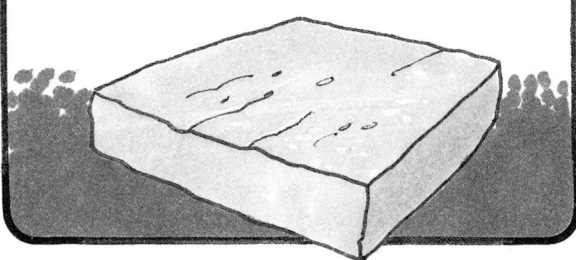

2 Carefully press the twig into the block, and then remove it, leaving the shape of the twig in the block. Smear grease around the surface of the block.

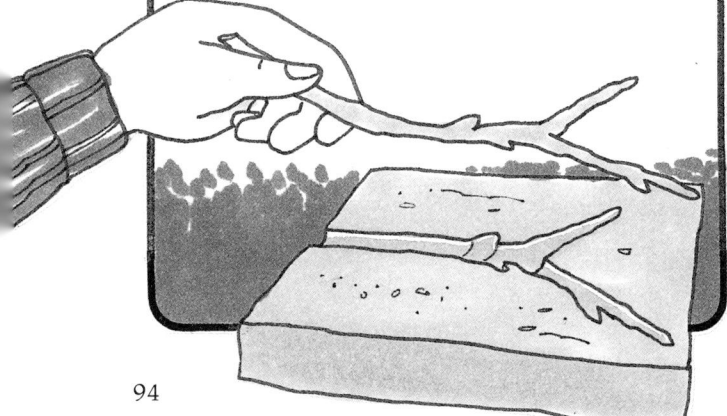

3 Tape cardboard around the block, as shown, being careful not to spoil the shape of the block.

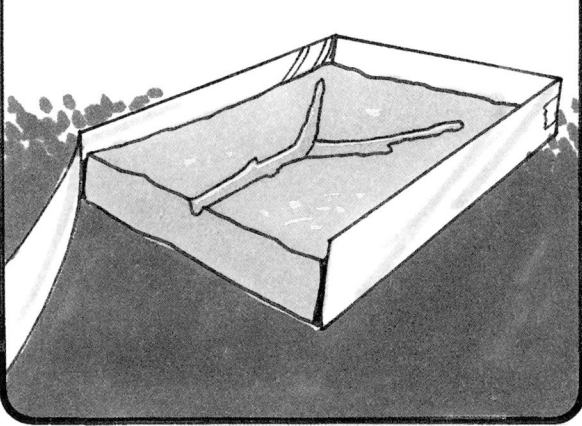

4 Mix some plaster of Paris with water, following the instructions on the packet (it should be creamy, but still possible to pour). Pour the mixture into the cardboard 'box', and leave it to set.

5 When the plaster of Paris is hard carefully remove the cardboard and the Plasticine block, leaving the plaster cast of the twig. You can now paint this if you wish.

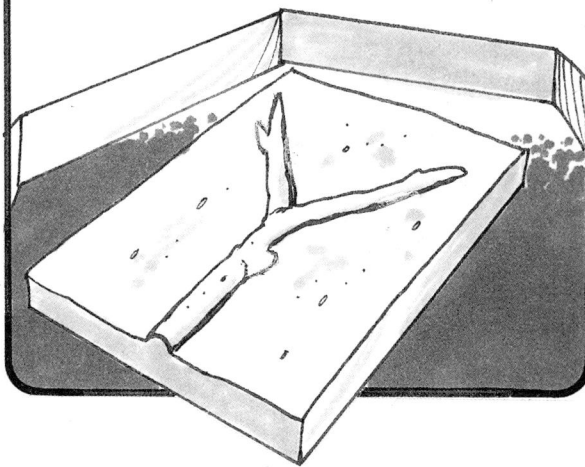

Make a plaster cast of a footprint

1 Find a suitable animal footprint from which to take the cast.

2 Tape a circle of cardboard around the print, carefully pressing the cardboard into the soil if possible.

3 Pour a plaster of Paris mix (creamy, but still possible to pour) into the cardboard ring.

4 When the plaster has hardened (you will need to come back the next day), remove the cardboard and gently lift the plaster away from the ground.

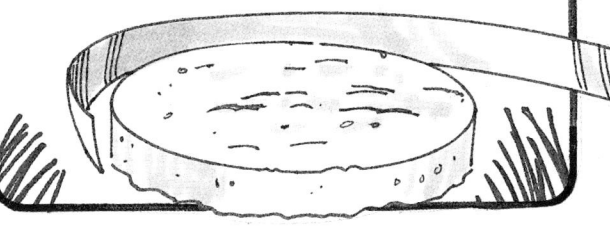

5 Carefully clean the surface of the cast and grease it all over.

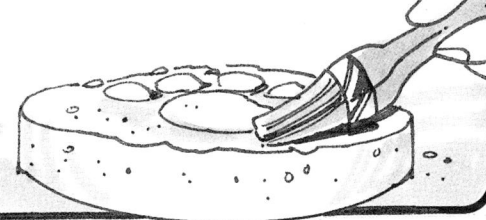

6 Place it, footprint upwards, and tape another ring of cardboard around it.

7 Pour more plaster of Paris on to the print, and when it hardens, carefully separate the two pieces. The final cast you made will be a replica of the print you found.

How tall is that tree?

Measuring the height of trees is easy when you know how. If you can measure the height of a tree, you can measure it the following year and see how much it has grown. Here is how to do it.

You Will Need
A pencil
A ruler or measuring tape
A friend

1 Ask a friend to stand against a wall and mark where the top of his or her head comes to. The distance from that mark to the ground will be your friend's height. Measure the height and make a note of it.

2 Find a tall tree, and ask your friend to stand next to it. Your friend should be the same distance from you as the tree is. Stand back about 12 metres from the tree and, with your arm outstretched, hold a pencil in line with your friend's body so that the top of the pencil is in line with the top of his or her head. Move your thumb down the pencil until it is level with the ground. The length from the top of the pencil to your thumb is equivalent to your friend's height, which you already know.

3 To find the height of the tree, all you have to do is see how many 'lengths' of this pencil are equal to the height of the tree, from where you are standing. Suppose that the number of 'lengths' is nine. If you multiply this by your friend's height, say 1.2 metres, you get the answer 10.8 metres. Therefore the height of the tree is 10.8 metres.

You can, of course, also use this method to find the height of buildings.

Read the story of a tree stump

You Will Need
A cut tree stump

Look closely at a cut tree stump growing preferably in a temperate region and the first thing that you will notice is that it appears to be made up of a series of rings – each one inside the other. These rings are called annual rings, and they represent the start of each new year's growth after the winter resting period.

Therefore, you can tell how old the tree was simply by counting the rings. But that is not all that the stump tells us, however. Sometimes the rings are wider on one side of the stump than on the other. This is because the rings are in fact made up of thousands of tiny tubes. Wider rings mean that the tubes are wider there. The wider tubes were produced on one side because the tree was growing faster there; that is it received more light, and took more water from the soil. Some rings will be wider all round than others. This is because the tree grew more in those years.

Occasionally you will see that the tree stopped growing altogether – perhaps it became diseased. You may also see blackened areas. The blackened area shows that the tree was damaged by fire or by lightning.

Make a permanent record of leaves and bark

One of the best ways to record leaves and bark is by taking a rubbing or print of them. There are so many different kinds of leaves and bark patterns that you will have no bother finding suitable subjects for your collection.

You Will Need
Thick white paper
A soft lead pencil or dark crayon
Boot polish
Blotting paper
Fresh leaves

To make a bark rubbing, hold a piece of paper against the tree trunk and go over the paper with a pencil or crayon. As you rub, the pattern of the bark will begin to appear.

To make a leaf rubbing, place a leaf with its underside (the ribbed surface) uppermost. Lay some paper over the leaf and go over it with a pencil or crayon until the pattern appears.

To make a leaf print, cover the underside (the ribbed surface) of the leaf with boot polish, using your fingers.

Place the leaf, ribbed side down, on paper. Place blotting paper over the top of the leaf. Rub gently but firmly on top of the blotting paper.

Remove the blotting paper, then carefully lift the leaf away to leave a coloured print on the paper.

☆ Have fun with leaves

Usually when leaves fall from trees, they are soon gone forever. You can preserve their appearance by making a leaf print (see page 99) or either a smoke print or leaf skeleton.

You Will Need
A few leaves
Vaseline or grease
2 glass jars
Non-toxic glue
White paper
A newspaper
A candle
A piece of card
An adult

2 Ask an adult to light the candle, then hold the jar over the flame until the whole outside is coated with carbon. (It will look grey.)

How to make a smoke print
1 Grease the outside of a glass jar. This will make sure that you get a good clear print.

3 Place a leaf, underside (ribbed surface) up, on a folded newspaper to act as a cushion and roll the smoky area of the jar over the leaf.

4 Put a sheet of white paper over the leaf, and roll again with a clean jar. The leaf details will appear on the paper.

2 Pound the leaf carefully with your fist so that all the dead cells between the veins crumble away and leave just the skeleton behind.

How to make a leaf skeleton

1 Choose a large, dead leaf, making sure it is very dry and brittle, and place it between two sheets of paper.

3 Glue the skeleton to the card.

☆ What is the gas given off by plants in sunlight?

In sunlight, green plants go through a process called *photosynthesis*. The leaves trap the energy of the sun and use it to drive a chemical reaction which makes food out of carbon dioxide (from the air) and water. During photosynthesis, the plants give off oxygen through holes in their leaves called *stomata*. We can prove that this is so, with this experiment.

You Will Need
A large jar
A small glass funnel
A test tube
Water
Pondweed (available from most aquarium stockists if you cannot find any in a pond)
2 small coins
A wooden taper
An adult

Set up the experiment as shown in the illustration. The test tube must be completely full of water to begin with. Immerse it in the jar of water and place it over the funnel, keeping the end of the test tube under water. Place the apparatus near sunlight or a warm place, and soon bubbles of oxygen will rise from the pondweed into the test tube, displacing the water that was in it.

To test for oxygen, ask an adult to light the wooden taper and then blow it out. Whilst the taper is still glowing, quickly remove the test tube (keep the mouth facing downwards) and place the glowing taper in the tube. It will relight with a 'pop' showing oxygen is present.

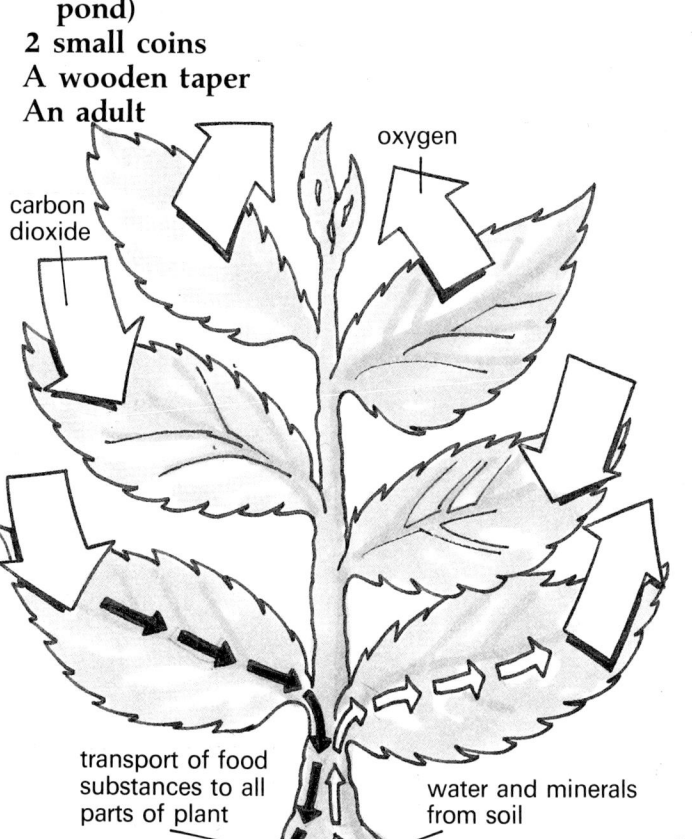

carbon dioxide

oxygen

transport of food substances to all parts of plant

water and minerals from soil

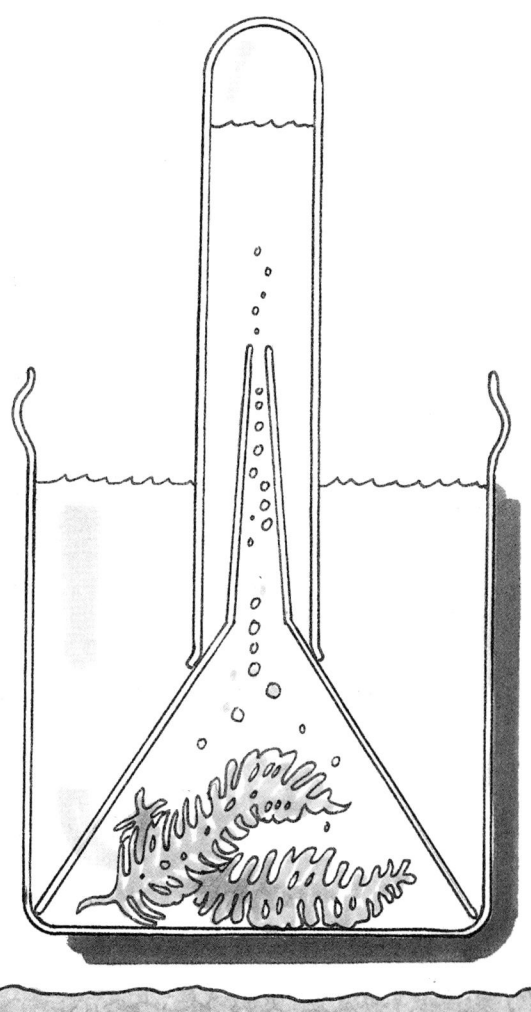

See how roots and shoots grow

You Will Need
A jam jar
Water
Blotting paper
Pea seeds

1 Soak the pea seeds in warm water for about two hours.

2 Line the inside of the jam jar with blotting paper, and add sufficient water to the bottom of the jar so that it rises and thoroughly wets the blotting paper.

3 Push the soaked pea seeds between the glass and the blotting paper. Leave the jar in a warm, light place.

In a few days the pea seeds will have started to germinate. In other words, the root will have started to grow out of the seed. After a couple of days it will be several centimetres long. Notice that as it grows it bends downwards. In nature, the root will always grow downwards into the soil. It is attracted downwards by a force called *positive geotropism*. It grows away from light and towards water which is, in nature, underground.

4 Turn some of the seeds around so that the roots point upwards. Leave them for a few more days, making sure that the blotting paper is still damp, and see what has happened. The roots refuse to grow upwards, but have instead bent over to continue growing downwards.

When the shoot starts to appear, it grows upwards by a force called *negative geotropism*. It grows towards the light. If you turn the jar on its side, the shoot will also twist round so that it continues to grow upwards.

103

Discover the growing region of roots

Does the entire root of a plant grow into the soil, or does growth only take place at a particular part of the root? You can easily find out.

You Will Need
Pea seeds
A jam jar
Blotting paper
A ruler
A sewing needle
Ink (The best sort to use is one which does not smudge when wet.)

1 Germinate some pea seeds. To do this fold a piece of blotting paper inside an empty, clean jam jar. Push a few pea seeds between the blotting paper and the sides of the jar. Thoroughly moisten the blotting paper and place it in a warm, light position. Keep the blotting paper moist. After a few days the roots will begin to appear from the seeds. When they have reached about 2.5 centimetres in length, you can begin the experiment.

2 Take one seed or more from the jar and, using a ruler, mark the root into 3-millimetre sections by making a tiny line on the root using the needle dipped in ink. Be careful not to damage the root as you do this.

3 Replace the seed in the jar as before. Each day measure the distance between the marks on the root. Did all sections of the root grow the same amount?

All parts of the root will have grown, but the bottom will have grown most as this is the growing region of the root.

What happens to the water in a plant?

You probably know that an actively-growing leafy plant must have water or it will die. But what happens to the water in the plant? In fact the water is constantly moving through the plant. It is drawn in through the roots, rises up the stem and passes out of the plant through tiny holes in the leaves called *stomata*. Evaporation of water from the leaves is called *transpiration*, and the whole process of water uptake and loss means that the plant's cells can always rely on a steady supply of water and vital chemicals (dissolved in the water) to enable it to grow. Here is how to demonstrate that this is what happens.

You Will Need
A small pot plant
A polythene bag
String

Place a polythene bag over a pot plant and secure the bottom of the bag with string. Put the plant in a sunny place. After a few hours see what has happened. The inside of the polythene bag is covered with tiny droplets of moisture, showing that the leaves of the plant are giving off water. Whilst this has been happening, the plant has been drawing on fresh supplies of water from the soil in the pot.

Curl a stem

You Will Need
A glass full of water
A stem and flower
A knife

Slit the stem into four strips as shown, and place it in the glass of water. The strips will curl up tightly. This is because the cells of the inside of the stem take up more water than the outside cells and expand as a result, causing the strips to curl. Normally, the continuous outer layer of cells prevents this.

Are there invisible spores in the air?

In the air, there are millions of tiny particles called spores, which, if they fall on suitable ground will grow into new fungi. They are so small, however, that you cannot see them with the naked eye. You can easily prove their existence, however, by providing them with something on which to grow.

You Will Need
A drinking glass
A saucer
A magnifying glass
A piece of stale bread

Place a small piece of stale bread on a clean, dry saucer and moisten it with a few drops of water. Now place the glass over the saucer.

After a few days the surface of the bread will be covered in darkish patches. These are the start of fungal colonies. They have grown from spores which settle out of the air. They may be bluish in colour, in which case the fungus is probably *Penicillium*; or they may be blackish, in which case it is probably *Rhizopus*; if they are whitish, it is *Mucor*. The colonies will continue to grow until all the goodness has been taken from the bread. Look at the fungi with your magnifying glass. Can you see the strands, known as *hyphae*, or the round spore cases?

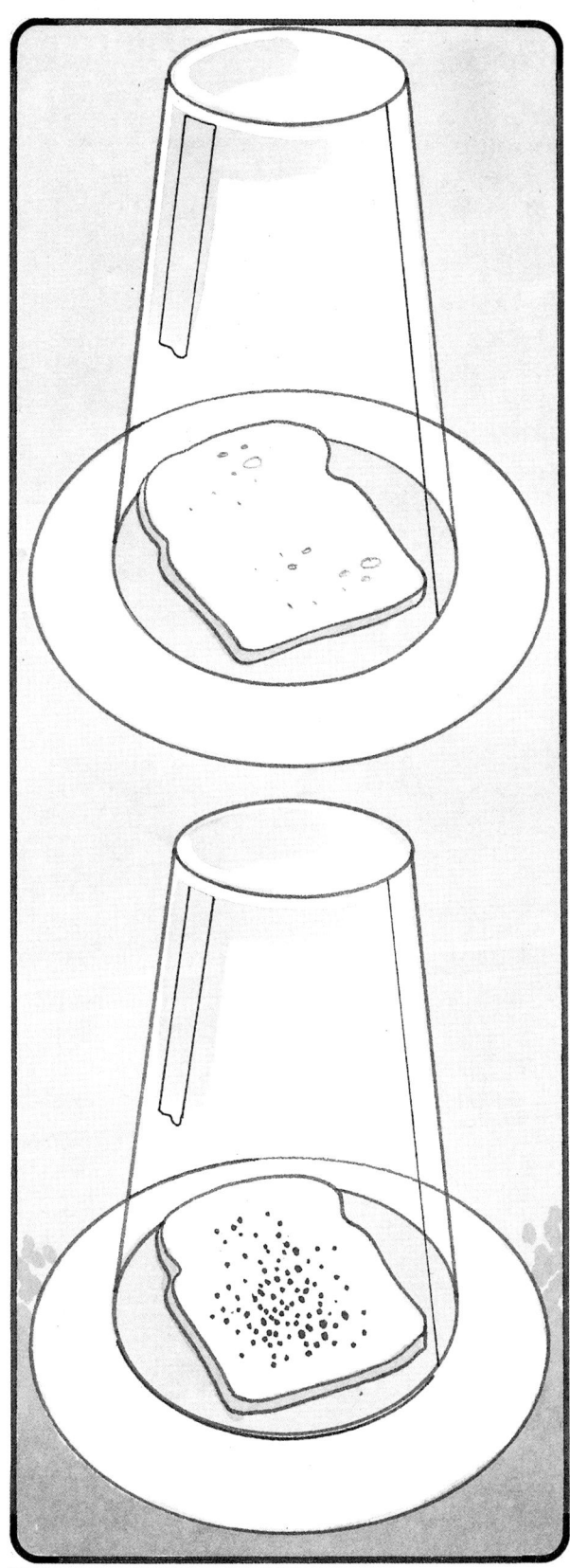

Repeat the experiment with orange peel, and see what fungi you get.

Make a spore print

Mushrooms and toadstools are the reproductive (fruiting) bodies of fungi. These fruiting bodies produce masses of tiny specks called *spores*. The spores are released from the mushroom or toadstool and, if they fall on suitable ground, they develop into a new fungus. Each fruiting body has its own spore pattern. You can see this pattern by making a spore print.

You Will Need
Sheets of white paper
A jam jar
A mushroom or toadstool (be very careful as some toadstools are poisonous)

1 Collect a mushroom or toadstool. Detach the cap from the stalk, taking care not to damage the delicate gills beneath the cap. (It is on the gills that the spores are borne.)

2 Place the cap, gills downwards, on to a piece of clean white paper. Place the jam jar over the cap to prevent it drying up or being disturbed.

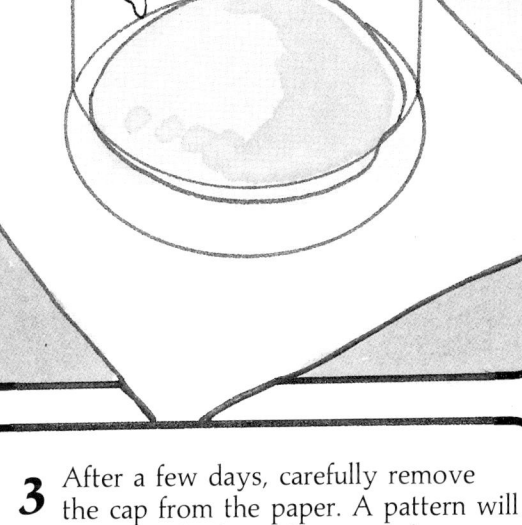

3 After a few days, carefully remove the cap from the paper. A pattern will have developed where the spores have fallen from the cap.

Study the power of osmosis

In nature, liquid from weaker solutions passes through living cell walls and mixes with stronger solutions. This is how water from the soil passes into the roots of a plant and is gradually distributed through the whole plant. This process is known as *osmosis*. Here is a way to demonstrate it.

You Will Need
A dish
Water
Sugar
Half a raw potato
A teaspoon

Scoop out a cavity in the half potato, taking care that you do not go right through it. Put the potato, hollow side upwards, in the dish containing some water, and note the water level on the potato. Now place a couple of teaspoonfuls of sugar in the cavity. Leave the experiment for several hours and then look at the water level in the dish.

The water level will have dropped. This is because the potato cells near the cavity have taken up the sugar, so increasing their concentration. This causes water from neighbouring cells to be drawn to them by osmosis, and these cells in turn take water from other cells. Eventually, the cells on the outside of the potato have to take up water that they have lost, and this they do by drawing on the water in the dish.

Test for starch and fat

You Will Need
A plate
Baking soda
A potato
A piece of bread
An apple
Iodine
A small piece of butter
Peanut butter or lard or cream
Lemon juice
Paper and pencil

Don't worry if you do not have all of these foods. You can still carry out the experiment with just one or two.

First, test to see whether food contains starch. Place a little baking soda on a dish and add a drop of iodine. Now add a drop of iodine to the cut potato. The spot where the iodine was added to the potato will turn dark purple, showing that starch is present in the potato. The baking soda does not change colour, because there is no starch in baking soda.

What happens if you add iodine to the cut side of the piece of apple, or any of the other foods?

Now test to see whether some foods contain fat. Draw a circle at each end of the piece of paper. Carefully rub lemon juice inside one circle, and butter inside the other. After about ten minutes, hold the paper up to the light and examine the circles. Look at both sides of the paper. The circle which was rubbed with lemon juice has started to dry; the lemon juice may even have disappeared completely. The circle which was rubbed with butter, however, still shows the greasy fat mark. It may even have started to spread through to the other side, and beyond the circle. Foods which contain fat will make paper greasy.

On a fresh piece of paper test to see whether peanut butter, or lard or cream, have fat in them.

Can you tell if something is a solution?

A *solution* is a liquid (usually water) with a substance dissolved in it. The molecules are so small that they cannot even be seen with a microscope. In a *colloidal suspension* one substance is suspended in another, and the molecules are large enough to reflect light, and make the direction of the light visible. Here is a way to tell a colloidal suspension from a solution.

You Will Need
2 milk bottles filled with water
Milk
A torch
Brown paper
Sticky tape

2 Put some sugar in one milk bottle, and let it dissolve. Put a few drops of milk in the other milk bottle.

1 Make a cone with the brown paper and tape it to the torch. This will cause the torch to throw a narrow beam of light.

3 Shine the torch through each bottle in turn. You will not see the light as it passes through the bottle with the sugar as this is a solution. But the light will be visible in the milky water proving that milk is a colloid. The milk is suspended in the water.

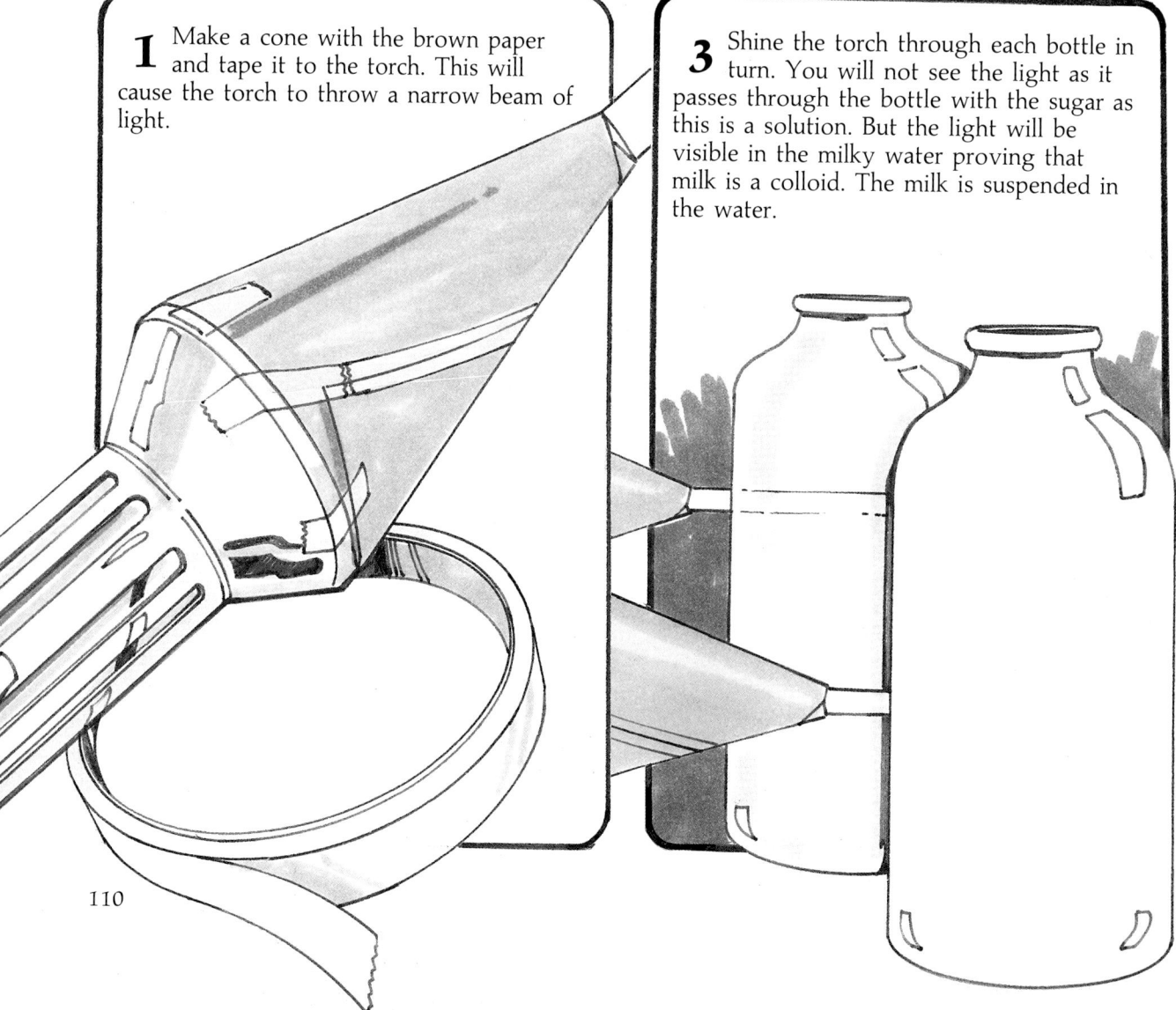

Does milk make water brighter?

You Will Need
A jar full of clean water
A few drops of milk
A torch

Shine the torch on to the top of the water in the jar. It is bright in the water, but the sides look dark from the outside.

Now add a few drops of milk to the water and stir. Shine the light into the jar again. This time, the jar appears brighter inside the water and much lighter from the outside.

This is because in clear water the light strikes the jar at such a small angle that a phenomenon called *total reflection* occurs, making the light 'stay inside' the jar. Once the milk has been added, the light hits the tiny particles of milk suspended in the water, and thus breaks up and is reflected out through the glass.

Demonstrate how energy can be transferred from one thing to another

You Will Need
Smooth surface, such as a table top
A ruler
2 coins of equal size
1 coin larger than the 2 equal sized coins
1 coin smaller than the 2 equal sized coins

Place the two equal sized coins side by side on the table. Place one end of the ruler in line with, but about 3 centimetres away from, one of the coins, with one end resting on the table. Hold the other end of the ruler in your hand so that it is at an angle of about 45°. Place the large coin on the ruler half way up. Let it go. It will slide down the ruler, strike the other coin and move it forwards. Energy was transferred from one coin to the other, making it move forward.

Now repeat the procedure, letting the smaller coin strike the other of the equal sized coins. Notice that this time the coin that is struck moves much less. This is because the lighter coin has less mass and is able to impart less energy (and hence movement) than the heavier coin.

Test gravity

It is said that the Italian scientist Galileo once performed an experiment in which he dropped stones of different weight from the Tower of Pisa. He discovered that they all reached the ground at the same time.

Here is a way to reconstruct his experiment, but using coins instead of stones.

You Will Need
A flat piece of wood, about 1 m long
Several coins of different weights

Place the coins along the piece of wood. Hold the wood above your head and stand on a chair if you like, then tip the wood so that all the coins fall together. Do your coins all reach the ground at the same time?

If you tipped the wood so that all the coins fell together, they will all reach the ground together. This is because gravity acts on everything equally, pulling them down at the same speed.

Test centrifugal force

Centrifugal force keeps an object moving in a circle as far away as possible from the centre of revolution. The faster the object revolves the greater the centrifugal force tending to 'throw' it outwards. This is why you cannot easily sit forwards in your seat when you are on certain fairground rides. Those that spin you and your seat from a central point are holding you in that position by centrifugal force. To demonstrate this, do this experiment – out of doors.

You Will Need
Small bucket of water

Put some water in a bucket – about one-third full is ideal. Hold the handle and swing it quickly over your head and down in a circle. Alternatively you can spin round on your feet and lift the bucket horizontally. In each case the water stays in the bucket, pushed towards the bottom by centrifugal force.

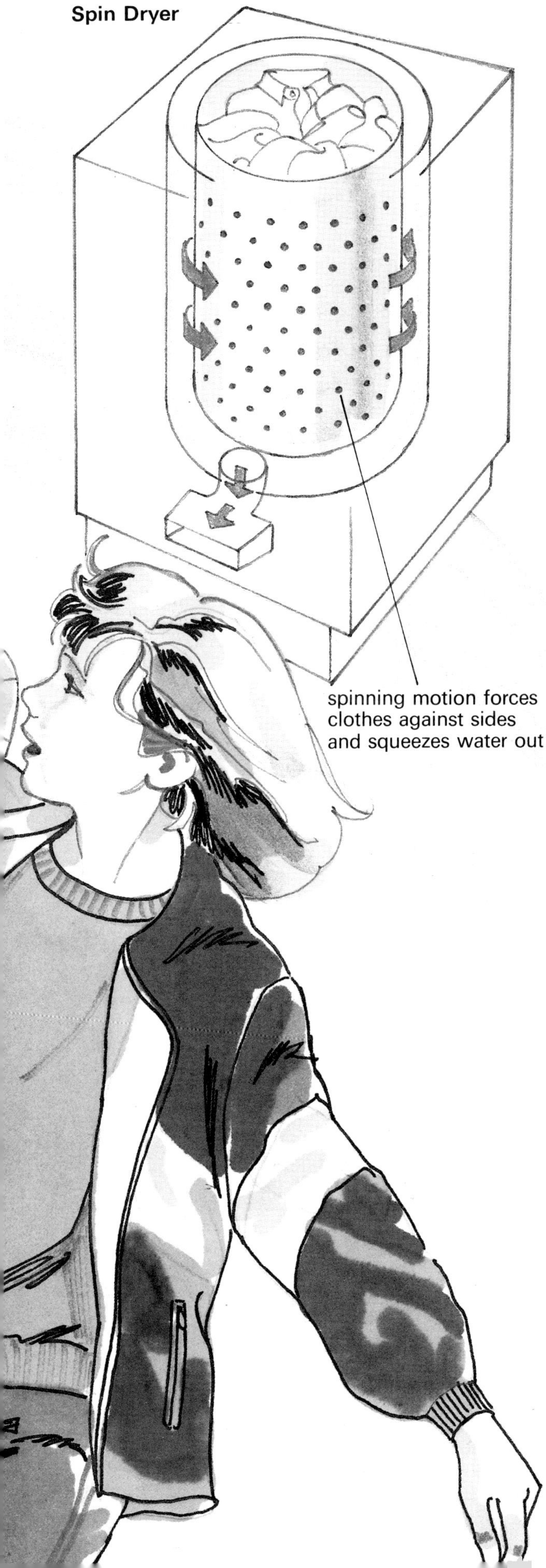

Spin Dryer

spinning motion forces
clothes against sides
and squeezes water out

Watch atoms in action

You Will Need
A watch or clock with a luminous dial
A strong magnifying glass

You need to do this experiment at night, or when it is dark. Turn out the lights and wait for about ten minutes so that your eyes become accustomed to the dark. Now look at the watch or clock dial by focusing the magnifying glass on it.

You will see flashes or sparks coming from the dial. This is because the dial is painted with luminous paint containing a radioactive substance called radiothorium. Atoms of radiothorium are constantly splitting and sending out particles. When the particles strike the zinc sulphide in the paint, they light up.

115

Make electricity

Most of the electricity we use comes from the mains or batteries, but there is another source called *static electricity* that we can generate ourselves. There are lots of ways of generating static electricity, and proving that something is charged with electricity. Here are some things you can do.

You Will Need
A nylon comb
Woollen cloth or piece of fur (an old fur glove will do)
A table tennis ball
A pencil or ruler
Tissue paper
Your pet cat (if you have one)

If you have a pet cat carry it into a cool dark room. Gently rub the cat's fur from the head down along the back for several minutes, always in the same direction. You will see sparks of electricity jump from the coat. You may hear the fur crackle, too. This will not hurt your cat, however.

Rub the comb vigorously with the woollen cloth or piece of fur. The comb is now charged with static electricity. Bring the comb close to the table tennis ball on a table. The ball will be attracted to the comb, and will follow it if you gently draw the comb away.

Rub the comb vigorously with the woollen cloth or piece of fur to charge it with static electricity. Place it near to (not touching) water which is trickling from a tap. Hey presto! The water bends towards the comb.

117

Make an electroscope

An *electroscope* is an instrument which detects the presence of positive or negative charges in objects. You can easily make one.

You Will Need
Tissue paper (about 2 cm × 20 cm)
Woollen cloth or piece of fur
A pencil or ruler
A nylon comb

1 Crease the strip of tissue paper across the middle.

2 Lay the paper on the floor crease up, and rub it with the piece of fur.

3 Hang the paper over the pencil or ruler. The ends will fly apart showing that they have negative charges. Now rub the comb with the fur and place that between the ends? Does your hand have the same sort of electrical charge as the rubbed comb?

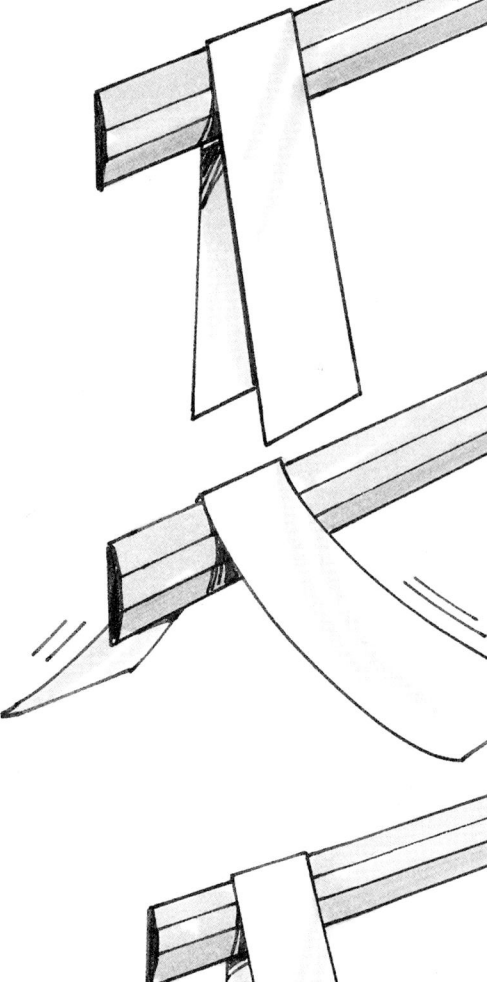

Here is a way to make a more elaborate electroscope.

You Will Need

A jar with a tight-fitting cork lid
A piece of copper wire
A piece of thin aluminium foil (chewing-gum foil with the paper removed will be quite suitable)

1 Make a hook in the end of the wire and push the wire through the cork.

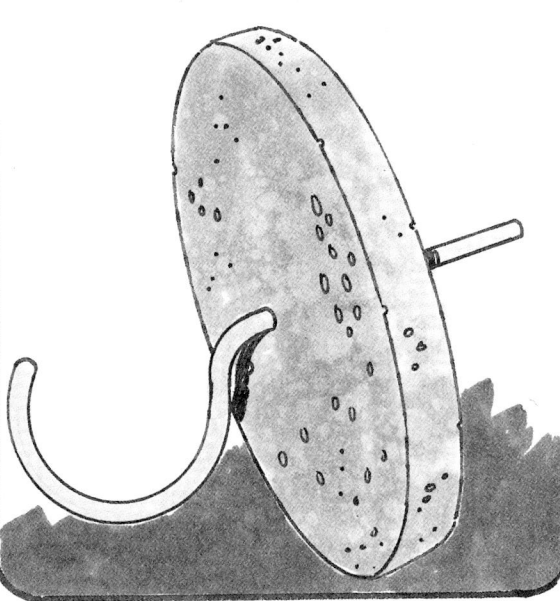

2 Crease the piece of foil, then hang it over the hook.

3 Push the cork tightly on the jar so that the hook and foil hang down inside the jar.

You only need to bring an electrically charged object like your rubbed comb near the wire for it to cause the foil to fly apart. If you touch the wire with your finger you discharge the foil, and the two ends will drop down again.

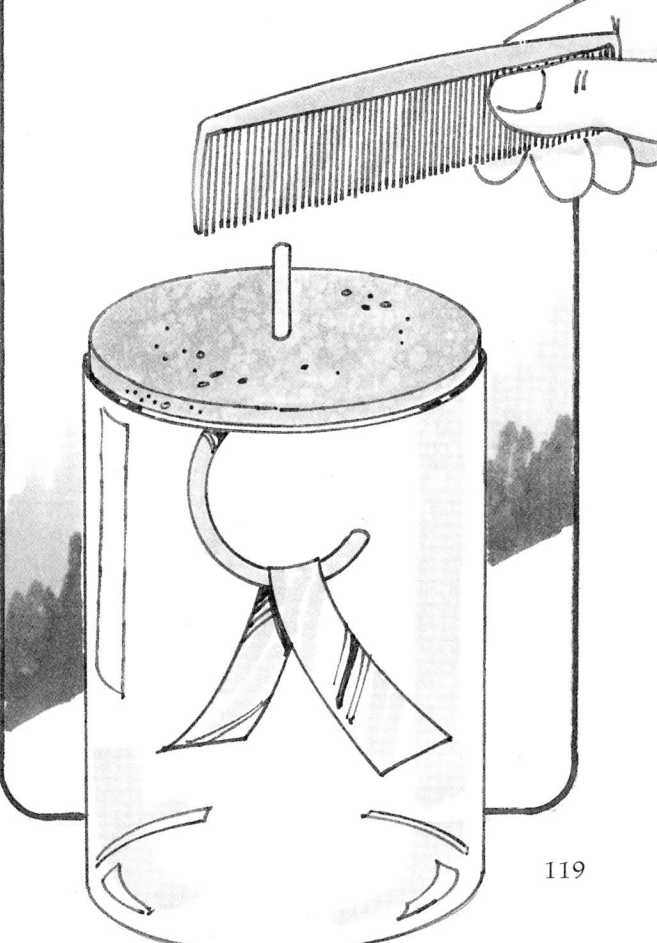

119

☆ Store electricity

Until about 200 years ago scientists who generated *static electricity* (not flowing within a circuit) were unable to store it ready for use. Then a device called the *Leyden jar* was invented, which could store static electricity. This is how to make a Leyden jar.

You Will Need
A wide-mouthed jar
Aluminium foil
Wire from a coat hanger about 20 cm long
Wire from a coat hanger about 12.5 cm long
A block of wood about 15 mm thick large enough to cover the mouth of the jar, with a small hole drilled through it
Non-toxic glue
Sticky tape
A nylon comb
Woollen cloth
5 paper clips
Bell wire about 1.5 m long
A drill
An adult

1 Bend one end of the 12.5-centimetre length of wire into a hook.

2 Ask an adult to drill a small hole through the wood. Then push the hooked wire through the hole. Secure the wire by squeezing glue into the hole.

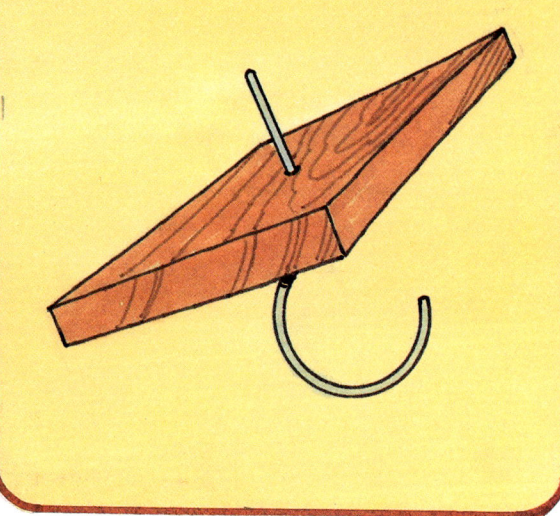

3 Line the bottom and lower half of the jar with aluminium foil, and glue it in place. Do this on both the inside and the outside of the jar.

4 Make a chain with the paper clips and hang this on the hook.

5 Place the wooden block, with wire hook and paper clip chain, on top of the jar so that the hook and chain are inside the jar.

6 Crumple some aluminium foil into a tight ball, and spike it on to the end of the wire.

7 Scrape the insulation off both ends of the bell wire.

8 Tape one bare end of wire to the foil on the outside of the jar, and tape the other to a metal tap or radiator pipe.

Now you have a Leyden jar. To charge it with static electricity, vigorously rub the comb on the woollen cloth. This will give the comb a negative electric charge. Touch the comb against the aluminium foil ball. Rub the comb again and touch the foil. Do this several times. The negative charges that you have generated will travel down the wire and collect in the bottom of the jar.

To discharge the jar, bend the 20 cm-long wire into a semi-circular shape and wrap several turns of sticky tape around the middle of the wire. Hold the wire by the tape and touch one end against the aluminium foil on the outside of the jar and, keeping this end in contact with the foil, touch the other end against the aluminium-foil ball. Just before the wire touches the ball a large spark will jump from the ball to the wire, showing that the electricity is discharged.

You can charge and then discharge your Leyden jar as often as you wish.

Make electricity from a lemon

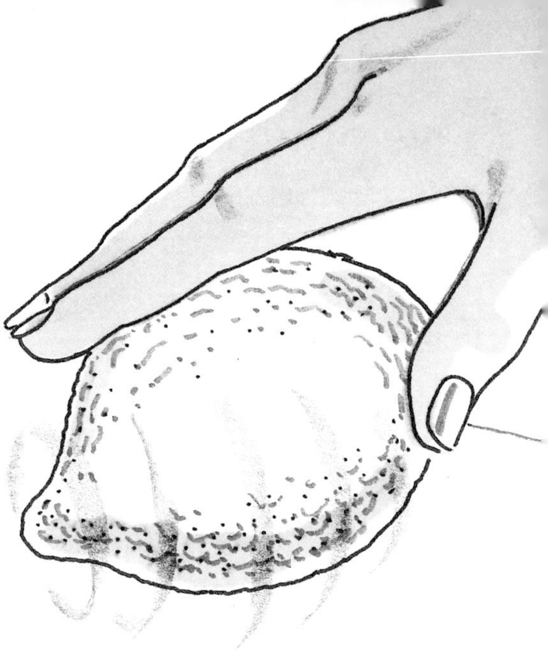

Believe it or not, a lemon can produce electricity. You can easily prove this by using the lemon to make a simple *electric cell*. An electric cell produces a current. The basic parts of an electric cell are strips of two different metals and a chemical called an *electrolyte* which conducts the current. The juice of the lemon acts as an electrolyte.

You Will Need
A lemon
A clean strip of zinc
A clean strip of copper

Roll the lemon to make it juicy inside. Insert the strip of zinc and the strip of copper into the lemon, leaving one end of each sticking out. Make sure that they do not touch each other inside. Now touch both the strips of metal at the same time with your tongue. (The zinc and copper should be very clean before you do this.) You will feel a slight tingling sensation which tells you a current is flowing.

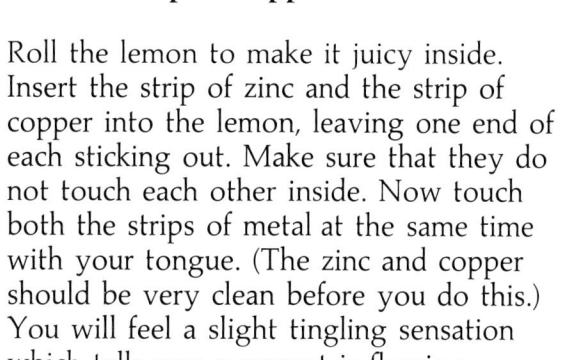

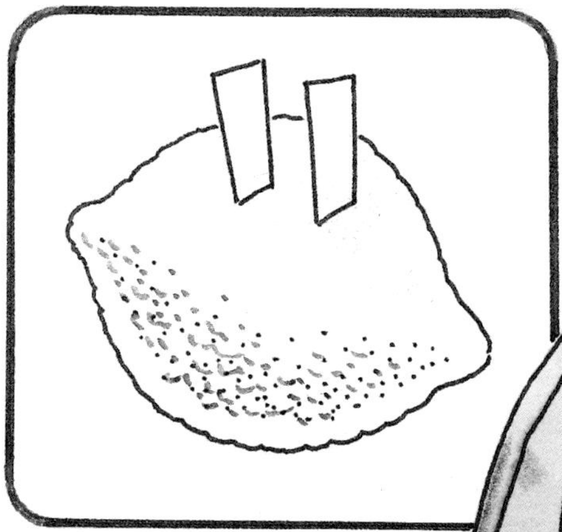

Have power over your friends

Ask your two friends to grasp a broomstick each, in both hands, and to stand about a metre apart. Tie one end of the clothesline near the top of one broomstick, and then wrap it around both sticks several times as shown.

Tell your friends to try to keep their sticks apart as you pull on the clothesline. Try as they may, they will not be able to prevent you from pulling the two sticks together.

How is this feat of muscle power achieved? In fact, it has very little to do with muscle power but a lot to do with the power of pulleys. By wrapping the clothesline around the broomstick you have created a system of *pulleys*, and a system of pulleys can move heavy loads. In this case the 'heavy load' is your two friends pulling on their broomsticks.

effort load effort load

Things learnt from these experiments

Everyone has a different pattern of ridges on their fingertips, and fingerprints are used for identifying people.

Your heart beats faster when you do something energetic.

Different parts of your tongue are sensitive to different tastes.

Some parts of your skin are more sensitive to touch than others.

Your blind spot is a part of the eye which cannot see.

Bones are made up of both hard minerals and soft tissue.

Reflexes are automatic reactions which the body cannot control.

Your reaction time varies according to the time of day, your age, whether you are tired, and many other factors.

Ice takes up more room than the water it is made from.

Things dissolve faster in warm water than they do in cold water.

Every action (such as steam escaping from a small hole) has a reaction (such as a movement in the opposite direction).

Water will evaporate more quickly from a large shallow container than from a small deep one.

The surface tension of water is strong enough to support a pin or a small insect.

Water climbs up a narrow tube because it is attracted to the sides. This is called capillary action.

The process of rusting uses oxygen from the air.

Cold water is heavier than hot water and will sink below it.

Lift on an aeroplane's wing is created by the decrease of pressure on the top surface as the air passing over it has to travel faster than the air underneath it.

Carbon dioxide can extinguish a fire.

Stalactites and stalagmites are formed by the constant dripping of calcium-laden water.

Pressure can cut ice by causing heat.

A compass uses a magnetized needle to point to North.

A solid such as wood or string will conduct sound better than air.

When light moves from one medium to another, eg from air to water, it is refracted (changes direction).

White light is made up of the colours of the rainbow.

Heat will move from a warm object to a cold one.

Some materials, such as metal, conduct heat better than others, such as wood.

Atmospheric pressure varies, and these variations are measured by a barometer.

Winds high above the Earth can blow in different directions from those at its surface.

Hair stretches or contracts according to the amount of moisture in the air.

Soils are made up of all sorts of different particles.

Earthworms mix the particles of the soil and allow air to reach the roots of plants by their burrowing.

Owls regurgitate pellets of the parts of their food which they cannot digest.

The rings on a tree stump can tell the life history of that tree by their number and width.

Plants create their food by photosynthesis, a process which uses sunlight, carbon dioxide and water, and gives off oxygen.

Negative geotropism causes seed shoots to grow upwards and *positive geotropism* makes the roots grow down.

Plants are constantly drawing water up through their roots, stem and leaves, and give it off to the air as vapour.

Spores are tiny particles produced by fungi and released into the air, and from which new fungi grow.

Water from soil passes into plant roots by a process called osmosis, in which liquid moves through cell walls from a weak solution to a stronger one.

A solution is a liquid with a substance dissolved in it, whereas a colloid is a liquid in which a substance is suspended.

Gravity acts on all objects equally, pulling them down at the same speed.